THINGS AND IDEALS

ESSAYS IN FUNCTIONAL PHILOSOPHY

BY

M. C. OTTO

DEPARTMENT OF PHILOSOPHY
THE UNIVERSITY OF WISCONSIN

NEW YORK
HENRY HOLT AND COMPANY

KRAUS REPRINT CO.
New York
1970

Reprinted by arrangement with Holt, Rinehart & Winston, Inc.
KRAUS REPRINT CO.
A U.S. Division of Kraus-Thomson Organization Limited

Printed in U.S.A.

2-26-79

To
THE MEMORY OF
MY MOTHER

PREFACE

THE twelve essays of this book are devoted to a cause. They are intended to help make articulate a social philosophy which recognizes equally the reality of things and ideals, and which aims to further their reciprocal interpenetration in the interest of human happiness. Possibly no one who writes on such a theme does anything at last but render into words a fantasy which, because of his particular angle of vision, glows with peculiar radiance. Even so, the present state of social idealism makes it desirable (since after all it may not be in vain) that any one who still clings to the hope of a better to-morrow make known, if he be so minded, the reason for the faith that is in him, and that he do so with all possible clearness and frankness.

People who insist upon being freed from the tyranny of "the many that change and pass," who absolutely refuse to seek in the world of change for the means of its redemption, as well as those who are set in their denial of the reality or efficacy of anything but things, will do well to save themselves the irritation of reading the pages that follow. The essays are meant for persons whose views are not as yet fixed in either of these extremes, persons who are in search of a method of combining aspiration with loyalty to fact. To such persons they may open a way to the development of a form of idealism free from sentimentality, yet steadfast in the refusal to accept the material order as the pattern of life.

Six of the twelve chapters were first published in periodicals. Chapters I and X appeared in *The American Review,* and are here only slightly changed. Chapters II, III, and XI (the two former now revised) were printed in *The Unpartisan Review.* A considerable portion of Chapter VIII was published in *The International Journal of Ethics.* A few paragraphs have been taken from the summary of an address delivered before the Ethical Culture Society of New York, published in *The Standard.* The editors of these journals have graciously permitted the present use of the material.

Since the book was completed, two men whose views are discussed—Jacques Loeb and A. Clutton-Brock—have died. I have permitted the material bearing on them to stand unaltered because the question was one of views, not of persons.

The notes grouped together at the end of the volume are intended for those who wish to follow up the problems considered. The reader may find there more or less detailed directions to the articles and books referred to in the discussion.

Unpretentious as this volume is, I must acknowledge myself under heavy debt for what it contains. To attempt to relate the story of these obligations would be a grateful occupation. It would revive happy, expansive hours lived in class rooms with teachers and students, in libraries with stimulating books, in fields and hills and marshes with friends of these and other years. And who shall say that the words one has read in books or heard from human lips have had more to do with the deeper meanings of one's thought than yellow moons and red suns, the wind in the pines, the silences under the stars?

It would be a grateful occupation, but the story would be too intimate and personal properly to have a place here. I cannot, however, forgo this opportunity to express my appreciation of the assistance of those who have been most directly connected with the preparation of the essays as they stand: to V. T. Thayer for helpful criticisms and suggestions; to Arnold Dresden for a careful reading of most of the chapters and a sympathetic but critical examination of the argument. With this help ambiguous passages were cleared up and the whole position strengthened. My largest debt is to one who would be pained to be mentioned, and so must remain nameless, but without whose intelligent devotion to the general project, and active, detailed attention to its statement, both as to content and form of expression, the result would have fallen much below the accomplished level, whatever that may be.

M. C. O.

CONTENTS

ix

"Those who do insist that the ideal and the real are dynamically continuous are those by whom the world is to be saved."

WILLIAM JAMES.

"If philosophers could aid in making it clear to a troubled humanity that ideals are continuous with natural events, that they but represent their possibilities, and that recognized possibilities form methods for a conduct which may realize them in fact, philosophers would enforce the sense of a social calling and responsibility."

JOHN DEWEY.

"Once more the trial must be made to realize the dream, to distill out of this little piece of cosmic stuff and this tiny stretch of time a strain of music, thrilling, glorious, and beautiful."

A. E. HAYDON.

"If thou seest a man of understanding, get thee betimes
    unto him,
And let thy foot wear the steps of his door.
Yet accept no person against thine own soul,
And let not reverence for any man cause thee to fall;
But let the counsel of thine own heart stand:
For there is none more faithful unto thee than it.
For a man's mind is sometime wont to bring him
    tidings,
More than seven watchmen, that sit above in an high
    tower."

ECCLESIASTICUS.

THINGS AND IDEALS

CHAPTER I

HAST ANY PHILOSOPHY IN THEE, SHEPHERD?

THERE is something exhilarating in the attempt of the philosopher to survey all time and all existence and to report the result in one all-comprising picture; to take stock of the universe and house all we know under one intellectual roof. For, taking us as we come, we know so little and so superficially. Chesterton may declare that every man has his philosophy, and that this is the most practical and important thing about him; James, Dewey, *et al.*, may generously endorse the saying, so that one would rather believe it than not; it is for all that an illusion. In point of fact what does this universally possessed philosophy come to? It comes to something having less kinship with anything to be called a philosophy than with the job-lot of odds and ends in Tom Sawyer's pocket. In so far as the vast majority of us are equipped with anything resembling an outlook upon life and the world it consists of a substratum of superstition about the supernatural, a smattering of social theory, a nest of group prejudices, a few wise saws, a rumor or two from science,

3

a number of slip-shod observations of life. To call this hodge-podge a philosophy is to take unwarranted liberty with language. No; the best that can be said is that, speaking generally, we are spiritually hungry and hanker after cosmic interpretations. It is this lack of philosophy which accounts for the ease with which any philosophic wind sweeps us off our feet.

These facts just now have a social as well as an individual application. Time was when a philosophy might be had if it was wanted. Both church and college stood ready to synthesize our knowledge; to supply men and women with a cosmology, a philosophy of history, and a plan of salvation. This "gave men a cosmic outlook," as G. R. Dodson says in speaking of the church view, "and some sense of the great frame in which human life is set, and most of all a profound sense that in this vast scheme our lives are significant. It was capable of dramatic presentation and afforded scope for the imagination, for poetry and religious feeling. As conceived and presented by the noblest minds, it also profoundly influenced the moral life. The outcome of the whole was to be a society from which was to be excluded whosoever loveth and maketh a lie, while even now the stars in their courses fight for righteousness, and those who stand steadfast in the truth feel that underneath them are the everlasting arms."

But "in the light of modern science," as he goes on to say, "this scheme has had to be given up." Mr. Dodson, in common with others, turns to Bergson's philosophy for spiritual renewal, but it is clear that no theological or philosophical scheme dealing with the meaning and purpose of life has been able to win the minds or hearts of men. A variety of new-thought movements has sprung up and may be said to flourish. Mysticism has experienced a vigorous revival in a number of different forms. Various modifications in theological and philosophical creeds have been proposed or adopted to meet difficulties presented by the intellectual presuppositions of the age. Yet it remains true that one of the marked characteristics of the time is the lack of any kind of total view. In philosophy as in life the few may be well to do, the many must live from hand to mouth.

Even this is a rosy description of the situation. It is coming to be suspected by those who think about such matters that philosophy, in the classic sense, is beyond the attainment of the few as well as of the many. Not that there is anything distinctly modern in a skeptical attitude towards philosophical accomplishment—far from it; the mood is ancient and ever recurring. But the contemporary doubt is not the old doubt. Socrates rejected the philosophies of his time because what was true in one was false in another, so that taken together they cancelled out. Kant was equally drastic in his day. Whereas every other science seemed to him to be steadily advancing, philosophy moved round and round in the same spot, never gaining a step. There was nothing to do but start over. In principle this is true of all the great speculators, of Descartes, Spinoza, Leibniz, Locke, Berkeley, Hume—to say nothing of more ancient or more modern representatives. To list them is to name men who erected their "marble temple shining on a hill" after having demolished the imposing shrines of contemporaries and predecessors.

All these attacks, however, were aimed at particular philosophical systems, not at philosophy itself. In this respect the contemporary challenge is new. The question now is whether there can any longer be anything like philosophy at all; whether in the face of the accumulation of human experience and the specialization of knowledge the man who, in Emerson's phrase, "takes up into himself all arts, sciences, all knowables as his food," who spares nothing, disposes of everything, has not become an impossibility. When we were told that Einstein's theory was understood by at most a dozen men in the whole world, many people smacked their lips in satisfaction. So the highbrow after all gets his just retribution! In general, however, we did not believe the report, or where we did, received it as an exceptional case. Yet Einstein is merely a striking example. Each of the sciences has assumed such scope that no individual worker in the field can master the various branches of his own science. Is it then to be thought possible for one mind to take a comprehensive view of knowledge as a whole? "There could be no Aristotle in the nineteenth century," said a noted British philosopher a score of years ago. Meanwhile the flood of detail which led him to make the remark has grown to something like a deluge, making it rash for us to expect even a Herbert Spencer in the twentieth century. In the light of this cumulative effect of man's thought and man's practice it seems a fair conclusion to many that philosophy, regarded as "the projection of a total vision of things," or the "effort to comprehend the universe, not simply piece-meal or by fragments, but somehow as a whole," must hereafter be received as pure fiction, and that the philosopher, instead of sitting supreme on the highest throne of knowledge, must wander in the by-ways of earth, singing with Nanki Poo,

> A wandering minstrel I,
> A thing of shreds and patches.

These conditions are reflected in the competing philosophic camps. The questions debated by contemporary philosophers center about the nature and function of philosophy. Behind these debates and responsible for them "lies the uneasy suspicion," as one of the debaters recently put it, "that all is not well with philosophy." And a crucial point at issue between those who would restore philosophy to health is whether the philosopher should aim at the final truth about the universe, with the further purpose of having this final truth serve as the basis of thought and conduct, or whether he should study life's concrete expressions, with the hope of suggesting a manner of human life in which the variety of men's aims might find active realization.

Moreover, whatever force the first alternative may once have had, it has little to-day. No one seems to take it seriously but certain philosophers. It is recognized by the plain man and by the specialist that universality of knowledge is no longer attainable by any mind. One scarcely reads a book in any special field which does not state this fact or imply it. A chemist, physicist, biologist, mathematician, who should announce that he had mastered the essentials of his field would be thought to have lost his balance. Everywhere it is admitted that the obstacles in the way of arriving at the essentials of knowledge in even a limited field and by those best qualified through training and experience to do so, are practically insuperable. If philosophers rush in where experts fear to tread what reception can they expect for the "total vision" with which they come out?

The philosopher may treat this fact cavalierly, but he cannot escape its consequences. If he aims to understand the world, "in principle, in general, and as a whole," and proposes to base this understanding upon the completest possible unification of knowledge, he is beset by the difficulty in multiple form. No philosopher has been able to surmount it, except in appearance. Here and there one has arrived at significant generalizations dealing with a particular domain of knowledge and has been recognized by specialists in that domain to have spoken with authority. But the claim to "a revelation of the whole universe, which shall be as coherent and complete as we can obtain" can hardly rest its case upon these achievements, great as they are. For the number of these conquests is strictly limited to one, or, at any rate, a few fields, and the mastery is in any case inseparable from direct occupation with the subject matter.

William James, whose astonishing range of insight might seem to furnish a refutation, supports the argument. There are fields that he did not touch; and he was at least artist, explorer, scientist (in several departments), and experiencer of states akin to religious ecstasy before he turned definitely to philosophy. His speculations are rooted in this fertile soil. Other well-known names might be adduced to the same point, to say nothing of the abundance of evidence supplied by philosophers of another grade, whose pretensions vary directly as the square of their ignorance, and whose unctuous deliverances on life, art, science, religion, music, anything you please, are saved from instant and general exposure by the verbal fog in which they muddle.

Suppose we admit, then, that the day is gone when a man might legitimately hope to act as umpire of ultimate truth. Does this leave any function for the philosopher to perform? One by one the special sciences, mathematics, biology, chemistry, physics, have left their common mother, philosophy; have set up independent households and become responsible for numerous progeny. Psychology, long a darling child, has all but slipped from the apron strings, while ethics, the favorite through the years, is showing a suspicious lack of interest in things about the house, and is looking more and more pensively out of the windows. It appears as if in our time all the children might get started in life for themselves. Is philosophy to be one of those good grandmothers who sits in the window by the geraniums, quietly folding her hands, dreaming of vanished days, and so awaiting the end?   It may well be.

But we have been thinking of philosophy as mastery of the secret of the universe, as the solution of the riddle of existence.   It has been differently conceived—by Socrates, for example.   It was defined long ago by Seneca as the guide of life, and recently by William James as "our more or less dumb sense of what life honestly and deeply means."   Especially during the last two decades has the conception of philosophy as a way of life rather than a theory of absolute reality won numerous adherents.   What if we follow this cue?

Well, first of all, mankind was never in greater want than now of a general theory of life and conduct, of some centralizing concept of life's meaning, of a *Lebensanschauung*.   It is everywhere conceded that the forces and institutions which heretofore served to rationalize endeavor have lost their grip upon men.   With a united voice we are declaring our spiritual bankruptcy.   And were we silent, events would proclaim the fact.   "Day unto day uttereth speech, and night unto night sheweth knowledge."   Nor is this a superficial aspect of the times.   It is not an "unbelief born of a greater belief."   We have lost our sense of direction.   This was becoming evident even before the catastrophe overtook us in 1914. There were signs in the air, like swallows before an approaching storm. The war, by increasing its momentum, made our drift obvious. An event of such proportions pushes men willy nilly out of their customary grooves of behaving, and so of feeling and thinking. For a time all this may be quite direct and spontaneous, but eventually self-consciousness supervenes, and when it does, men find themselves in a world topsy-turvy.

This spiritual collapse is the philosopher's opportunity. He may devote himself to achieving a new ideal. Without pretending to say that there is but one end to which the philosopher may devote his energies, here, at any rate, is an end worthy his best powers. From one point of view our bewildered and disillusioned state is most inopportune. It overtakes us in an era of history unique for its will to live forward—just when the need for guidance is exceptionally great. But the situation wears another face when viewed from a different angle. We then perceive that the present offers an unusual opportunity for the realization of a new and better manner of life. If the extraordinary vital energy seeking effective means of expression in the world to-day can be brought to make common cause with intelligence and good will, if impulse and reason can be correlated, the result will be of incalculable benefit to mankind. We have heard much in recent years of a crisis in civilization. The crisis is real enough, and it is this: Will man accept his present spiritual poverty as in the nature of things, or will he recognize it as the chance to win for himself the most promising orientation of life yet known? Let philosophy be dedicated to conceptualizing the latter alternative and to promoting the spirit necessary to its realization in fact. What calling can then be more important or more noble?

Not that philosophers have shown no interest in the problem of the good life. They have indeed. But their interest has taken a peculiar turn. "The philosopher," as Papini says, "desires to see the world issue and unfold, like a gigantic plant, from one simple seed; or seeks to trace all appearances of variation back to some vague primordial mystery wherein reason may find a certain pleasure, though sense be lost." Not to succeed in this is to fail utterly. If a philosophic position, for example, is chargeable with being dualistic, the author of it is expected to cover his face with his hands and leave the scene in confusion.

This bias philosophers have brought with them into the ethical field. It has been their habit to make the conception and realization of the good life inseparable from apprehension of the ultimate truth. Finite experience they have found too fragmentary, transitory, and dumb to offer any guidance—what was there left to do but turn one's back upon it and search for something of absolute and immutable worth from which the concept of the good life might be deduced with logical finality? Various as the formulations of this supreme principle have been, they have agreed in disparaging man's native interest in the common concerns of life. And so instead of the great principle being the servant of man, man has been made the slave of the great principle. Having rejected everything finite to begin with, the searchers have ended by discovering the good of goods in contemplation of the ostensible ultimate—the boundless, changeless, absolutely harmonious real, or in the sheer indulgence of their cosmic wanderlust.

The value of the philosopher to the community of the future depends, I believe, upon his ability to free himself from this tradition. Can he execute an about face? Can he satisfy his bent for comprehensiveness and depth in and through the issues of life, transitory though they be? That is the question being fought out in philosophy to-day, and upon the outcome hangs the destiny of the philosopher. It is doubtless true that we look in vain for an ideal of life in the world of matter, and that the wants of individuals are capricious. But material things and capricious wants do not exhaust the alternatives. We can rise above the standpoint of matter and of caprice yet keep our feet on earth. The philosopher, if he will, may be our friend and guide in this adventure. He may study man's capacities and frailties, the sources of his power and the causes of his weakness, the ideals that move him to action, the social institutions he has adopted or dreamed of, the natural environment which is at once his obstacle and his opportunity, with the aim of projecting a vision of society in which men might hope to be most freely, fully, and joyously alive. In a word, he may be prophet of an appealing possibility, rather than judge of ultimate truth.

The objection will at once occur that ideals unrelated to fact are chimeras. Which is true, but not pertinent. The philosopher must indeed be informed, and in the broadest and profoundest sense. He can have nothing in common with those free-ranging intellects which, in Mill's phrase, are "unprejudiced by any knowledge of the facts." But he must be informed in matters relevant to the human drama and its stage setting, not in the intricacies of the cosmic machinery behind the scenes or the purposes of the ultimate playwright. For facts are not his end, but his beginning. They serve him as mate-

rial out of which to fashion a vision of things to be—
to be if those who know the art can embody his vision
in forms concrete, and congenial to life. Philosophy
may serve the future as a source of ideas and suggestions, of moral inspiration and power.

The conception may be put in another form. We
live in a world where two things influence behavior,
facts and values To be alive is to aim at the attainment of ends, and this involves adjustment to conditions, knowledge of facts. But no one is indifferent to what ends are most worth attaining. Men desire to attain the ends most desirable. Even on the
plane of every day life, therefore, all men reflect on
facts and values. Nor is this all. Few men are limited to this naïve level. Few men are utterly without
some criterion of fact and some standard of value,
however vague, circumscribed, and contradictory
these may be, to which they mean to conform. Science, art, religion, and other disciplines enlarge and
deepen this reflective activity. They present new
worlds of fact; they embody particular values.

The question naturally arises (especially as life
increases in tempo and complexity) whether it is possible to attain to a view of life in which the values
represented by the specialized disciplines, and ultimately the wants of men, find adequate and harmonious recognition; a view of life which at the same

time is not a fanciful theory, but a workable concept, based upon a rigorous study of relevant fact.
And in so far as this is possible it represents the function of philosophy. Philosophy is to develop, as far
as lies within man's power, what may be called a
science of human values.

As a pioneer, then, in the search for the City of
Man the philosopher may render a service of great
value to his fellows. He may do another service,
equally vital and closely related to this. He may
help men to liberate themselves from their idolatry
of the familiar. He may rescue them from their
inveterate provincialism, and nurture in them a free
mind. We are accustomed to endorse the words of
a great spirit who said, "Know the truth, and the
truth shall make you free." Yet what do we fear
more than truth? We repeat the words, but what
we mean is, Believe this dogma, support this enterprise, vote this ticket, live according to this program,
—in short, accept this prejudice or be anathema.
Many an illegitimate offspring of the mind has thus
been elevated to a position of dignity and power
which, but for this slogan, would have wandered as
an outcast in a world of cold indifference.

It is this narrowness of spirit, which undermines
our search for truth even while we protest our loyalty to it, that the philosophic spirit may do some-

thing to correct. The first and perhaps fairest flow-
ering of philosophy was the outgrowth of a determination to replace tribal, national, racial habits of
thinking by a comprehensive view, and the habit of
telling tales about the world by observation and reasoning. Breadth of outlook, scope of sympathy, objectivity of judgment, devotion to truth—these were
the aim of the first philosophers. And this temper
or disposition, this willingness to let the mind range
freely about all sides of a subject, even the idols of
the soul, with no hope of reward but insight, is still
one of the best fruits of philosophy.

Perhaps the most stubborn bias in the way of the
free mind is the deep-rooted notion that the universe
has special reference to man and his affairs. To be
sure many have grown bold enough to smile with
John Fiske at the "quaint conceit" of the middle ages,
that unless the earth occupied an immovable and central place in the stellar universe human life could
have no meaning. Some have the courage to take
the next step with him, too, and insist that "zoölogi-
cally speaking, man can no longer be regarded as a
creature apart by himself," but must take his place
in the catarrhine family of apes. Few, however, will
go further. The vast majority will shrink, as Fiske
did, from considering humanity as a local incident in
nature, They will contend that man is the culminat-

ing goal of a divine energy which neither slumbers nor sleeps, and that on this foundation and no other can a purposeful life be built.

Philosophy has power to cure this astigmatism. I do not mean that philosophy is necessarily irreligious, or that its function is to prove man a waif in the cosmos. I mean that it sets the human venture in perspective. Through the appreciation of his utter insignificance when viewed under the aspect of the universe a man reaches mental maturity. He adds that flavor of imagination to his religion and that sympathetic understanding to his morality which, though certain simple souls have it by nature, is needed by most men to save them from pedantry or fanaticism on the one side and sentimentalism or cant on the other.

The philosopher may count in still another way. He may do something to protect us, through the function of criticism, from a ready acceptance of the sweeping, one-sided generalizations that periodically seep into the popular mind from the mind of the expert, and inhibit or divert men's spontaneous interest in a better world. Economic interpretation of history, mechanistic interpretation of life, survival of the fittest, behaviorism, determinism, materialism, nothing succeeds like success, self-preservation is the first law of life, and concepts of similar nature, though rarely examined and often unconsciously avowed, play a significant part as determiners of life conditions. The philosopher is at home in this field. He has specialized in world-views. He knows their rival claims, the grounds on which they rest, the weaknesses opponents have found in them. He is qualified to assist us to a truer estimate of their value than we are apt to get without his critique. So doing, he not only saves us from the danger and defeat of one-sidedness but adds a new dimension to our mental and emotional stature.

The philosopher, moreover, is a student of the theory of evidence, of methods of acquiring knowledge and estimating its logical worth. Philosophy thus sharpens judgment. It heightens appreciation of well-grounded conclusions and increases the power to detect fallacious or superficial reasoning. The philosopher, therefore, is able not only to direct us to material necessary for basic criticism of life, but to promote among us the desire and the ability to support fundamental beliefs with adequate grounds.

Viewed in this light who can doubt the value of philosophy as a function of life? Living as we do in a world where the demands made upon us are constantly mounting in number, and where the tempo of life is steadily accelerating, we are inclined to forgo reflection altogether. We are too busy keeping the pace to ask whither. Yet it is obvious that no age was ever more in need of asking whither than ours. And while life, having its inescapable practical aspect, demands short-range idealists, men and women who can invent the means of social improvement that promise immediate applicability, we shall fall far short of our possibilities, and make the work of these idealists futile in the end, unless we have a place of opportunity for long-range idealists as well, men and women whose minds are stretched to catch a glimpse of the Great Society to come, where sanctity of life, beauty of surroundings, and creative opportunity shall be a general fact.

It is common for those who are busy with the immediate triumph of ideas and those who seek the longer vision to have little patience with each other. They are equally indispensable, and are only a hindrance when they confuse their function. Bread must be baked. But bread without aspiration is vanity, and aspiration without intelligence is blind. Philosophy can bake no bread, neither can it define the channel of life. Philosophy can, however, break up "our caked prejudices," expand our mental and emotional horizons, stimulate us to think objectively and believe greatly, swarm our environment with ideas and ideals, and thus help us to project a glowing vision of joyous and beautiful things that might be done on earth. Our present consciousness of spiritual poverty, and the radical discord among contemporary philosophers are good omens. They assure this conception of philosophy, urged as it is in various forms, a fair hearing.

CHAPTER II

THE TWO IDEALS

IF we may trust those disconcerting gentlemen, the psychologists, it appears to be established that the world which we inhabit as adults, the richly diversified world of cities, fields, rivers, mountains, clouds, animals, people, and other things innumerable, is not at all the world into which we were born. According to these disturbers of the psychic peace, Stevenson was not speaking for the very young child when he wrote,

> The world is so full of a number of things
> I am sure we should all be as happy as kings.

For the environment of the baby, they say, is a colorless, meaningless, characterless vapor of feeling; or, as William James expressed it in one of his inimitable phrases, a "blooming, buzzing confusion."

One of the early tasks, then, which the seemingly helpless little immigrant has thrust upon him is the godlike one of forming a world out of chaos. And the most immediate problem, that of keeping soul and body together, having somehow been solved, a beginning is soon made on the job of sorting out the grand mix-up. Indeed, finding a place to get meals is itself the beginning of the process. So early is it demonstrated that to live to a purpose, one must live.

What could be more fascinating, if it were possible, than to observe just how the world of the adult, with all its variety and contrast, with all its laws and relatedness, little by little takes shape out of a psychic nebula? Alas, we are left entirely to speculation, or at best to risky analogy. Great as the triumph of science has been, no trail has yet been found to the land of forgotten days.

Think of some of the things we can do. We can determine the chemical composition of stellar bodies so far removed in space that we lack means of conveying an appreciable idea of their distance. We can detect organisms so small that when a drop of blood containing them is diluted five million times they are still present in sufficient numbers to affect an organism injuriously if a bit of the liquid be introduced into its blood. We can tell the story of organic evolution back millions of years beyond the first appearance of man upon earth, and we can predict thousands upon thousands of years in advance changes that will ultimately overtake our globe. Marvelous achievements, these, which would have held spellbound not only the Greek philosophers on the Ægean, but the Greek gods on Olympus. Nevertheless, our babyhood, the period of our lives when laboriously we laid down the first broad foundations of the world we now very largely take for granted, remains an unrecovered country, to whose bourne no traveler returns.

Well, however the world may come to be for the child, no distinction is at first made in it between fact and fiction. Everything is accepted on the same footing; all experience is of one tissue. Witches, fairies, giants, and all the creatures of irresponsible fancy have the same status as substantial things like cookies, toys, dogs, people. The kitten on the hearth-rug is real, but so is the cat of the wet, wild wood, that walks by himself, in all places alike. Out of doors is real, but so is the wonderland of Alice, and the world Jack discovered when he climbed the bean-stalk. Equally real are Cinderella, Little Red Riding Hood, the Dong with a Luminous Nose, the Cow That Jumped over the Moon, and a rich assortment of others. They all *are*, and the question of *what* they are has not arisen. In this golden age the lion of fact and the lamb of fancy lie down together.

But not for long. In a world like ours, such pure democracy of interest, such equal hospitality to every

form of experience, is not maintainable. And here
at least we have an explanation. The thirst for
knowledge closes the gates to paradise. To say that
a child is in a world is to say that a world exists as
a challenge to a child, a challenge to its curiosity and
its desire for mastery. Bacon has received much
credit for teaching men that knowledge is power,
but children knew it long before Bacon, and have
never forgotten it. In true Baconian fashion they
face their world in the spirit of interrogation, determined to find a way to desired ends.

Knowledge is power, but knowledge is disillusion.
Growing curiosity, enlarging experience, increasing
skill in observation soon bring contradictory beliefs
into juxtaposition, with the result that a revision of
beliefs, and then a fundamental reconstruction of the
world, become necessary. And the first far-reaching
reconstruction is the division of things into real and
make-believe. It is impossible to mark the hour
when this sophistication begins, for intellectual skepticism steals into childhood as dawn moves over the
rim of night. But we are not without experiences
which are typical of the process, although themselves
of a more or less developed type.

A young Missouri surgeon tells this story: "I remember," he says, "that when I was between five
and six years old, and lived in a small town in Illi-

nois, I had an interesting experience. Some weeks before Christmas our one drug store displayed a drum in the window. I wanted it badly. Having written to Santa Claus, as my parents suggested, I stopped daily in front of the window to admire the drum, and my desire for it grew until as Christmas drew near I could think of little else. Would Santa Claus bring me a drum like it?

"Sure enough, on Christmas morning there she was! When the first rush of joy had spent itself, and I was examining the drum, I noticed that it was exactly like the drug store drum, even down to a slight defect in one of the rims, and a small dent in its yellow tin side. This somehow made me wish to compare it, and I marched off to the drug store window. The drum was gone! I don't know why, but like a flash came the thought that my drum was the very drum I had seen in the window for weeks. Then how could Santa Claus have brought it from the North the night before? I have forgotten what explanation my parents gave, but it didn't satisfy me. I was sure that there was something wrong. I did not settle the point at once, but I felt, vaguely and yet really, that I had been missing something, and that I must keep a better watch on things. And so there came into existence a new boy who stood off and watched. Before long not only had the great team of reindeer been permanently stabled, but I had concluded that there weren't any giants and witches, just as there wasn't any Santa Claus."

In some such manner the child arrives at the profound distinction between fact and fiction, between a real world and a world of make-believe, and determines not to mistake the one for the other. The world which antedates the distinction is so intrinsically different from the one which succeeds it, and the individual has become so fundamentally changed in the process, that having once really crossed this Great Divide it is practically impossible to go back again even in memory or in imagination. All of us, however, were such monists, or believers in one form of reality, in the beginning, and we became dualists only when the subtle development of our critical faculties, or a flagrant contradiction in our beliefs, compelled us to revise our judgment of reality. Rejecting a world of one stuff, we accepted some experiences as true, and some as not; which, had we been philosophers, and thus able to invent terms such as Reality and Appearance, might have got us a great reputation.

Interesting and important as this phase of development is on its own account, it gains in significance when recognized as a stage in the progressive evolution of a new world and a new self. Differentiation

between fact and fiction is a big step in sophistication, but the fanciful is not the only imaginative element intimately incorporated in the child's universe.
There is also what the adult calls the moral ideal.
To the adult the moral ideal is the substance of
things hoped for, but to the child the "ought" is as
substantial as the "is." Men and women think in
terms of a moral order distinct from the concrete;
not so the child. To the child the wrongness of
lying is as real as the wetness of water. He takes
chances with lying, but so he does with water. And
while the discrimination between fact and fiction,
once achieved, makes a life of intellectual innocence
forever impossible, it does not, except in rare cases,
disturb moral beliefs. On the contrary, even while
the rift between the real and the make-believe becomes constantly broader and deeper, and the primacy
of the real ever more unquestionable, the expanding
environment, in home, playground, school, and
street, is persistently insinuating new imaginative
elements—ideals of conduct, of character, of citizen-
ship—into the world of accepted reality. Once
more, however, enlarging experience gives rise to a
conflict of beliefs; and conflict of beliefs, to the di-
vorce of what had hitherto dwelt together in harmony. Again there is no saying just when, but
sooner or later the growing child finds himself in

an ambiguous environment, and is forced to reconstruct his world and to become a new self. The following record of such a change is characteristic, although it usually comes earlier:

"I was between thirteen and fourteen years of age," writes a lawyer friend, "when for the first time the suspicion definitely entered my head that right and wrong were not ultimate realities like laws of nature, but rules invented by older people for children. It came about in this way. I lived in a small Wisconsin village, and my hero was the locomotive engineer of the scoot which ran between our village and the main line. Well, one day when I was getting some kerosene in a shed at the back of our general store, and he was sitting with some farmers' hired help about the big stove, I heard my hero say, 'Oh, of course, it's me for the straight and narrow around here. But there ain't a fellow of you'd have the nerve to follow my smoke in Chicago.' I remember how instantly the whole thing was clear to me: that he lived two lives, one for the benefit of the village, and another, more to his liking, in the big city. I don't know how I knew that the latter was not according to the moral code. Perhaps it was because in villages the wickedness of big cities, rather than anything else, is most advertised. At all events, my hero fell. Often since then I have wondered whether the faces I saw about the stove as I went out were transformed by an incipient despisal aroused by the overheard remark, or whether I had simply never observed their coarseness before. They looked different, and I felt an unmistakable antipathy not unlike that toward things unclean.

"The incident might have passed into memory, as the discovery of other moral delinquencies had doubtless done, without any serious effect upon the foundations of my moral world, but for some reason it didn't. Somehow the thought flashed into my mind (I am uncertain just how long after the experience with the engineer) that perhaps moral rules were like Santa Claus and fairy tales, things which you implicitly believed until you reached a certain age, when you see into them. I became skeptical. I kept eyes and ears open, and the more I observed and thought about it, the better the hypothesis appeared to fit the facts. Before long I passed the theory on to my chum. To my surprise he also was armed with observations calculated to show that what our elders taught us to be of paramount importance was more lightly regarded by themselves. I seemed to experience a marked expansion of individuality by virtue of this insight. What my discovery might have led to I cannot tell, for about that time a little dark-eyed maiden became the all-absorbing interest, and my adoration for her revalued all values. But that is really not part of this story."

Not every boy has his moral eyes opened in just this way. Some experience no specific moral crisis, and many become moral doubters through imitation, or through the encouragement of the more worldly-wise. In most cases, perhaps, the urge we call life pushes the individual into actions which violate hitherto accepted standards, and moral skepticism is a gesture of self-defense. Differences in detail but identify in principle. Experience coming into contradiction with experience, belief opposing belief, then some manner of readjustment, a new world and a new self, that is the universal record.

Childhood and youth are after all sequestered in a delectable valley, protected from the raw wind and weather of the work-a-day plateau. The year's at the spring, when rains are omens of promise and storms are soon out of breath. Troubles and disappointments are profoundly real—never more so—but they are fleeting, and duration is nine-tenths of pain. So these early defeats and readjustments do not permanently disturb the blue-sky outlook. Life, however, does not permit us to remain in the valley; it pushes us, pulls us forth; and disillusions overtake us in the way. We hope, and are disappointed. We trust, and are deceived. The glowing goal, in realization, turns to ashes. We would change the ordinary weeds of life for a garment more becoming to its worth and dignity, but life prefers squalor and rags. We are thwarted by wickedness in high places and weakness in low. We lay dear forms away in the earth drenched by gray rains in the night. Gradually, the assurance so companionable to youth that life has some great hidden meaning, becomes a friend estranged. What is it to grow up but, among other things, to learn that the world is not what we had thought it to be?

No man escapes disillusion, although there are differences of degree. And all men triumph over disillusion, but not in the same spirit. The familiar story of Jesus on an exceedingly high mountain, shown the kingdoms of the world and the glory of them, and confronted with the alternatives of great possessions or loyalty to spiritual vision, symbolizes human experience. The choice of the Galilean, however, is not the usual choice. The many hurry down to possess themselves of goods in the world newly discovered. They revise a well-known Biblical admonition, and say: "Lay up for yourselves treasures on earth, where moth and rust doth corrupt, and where thieves break through and steal. For where your heart is, there let your treasure be also." They not only enter the world, but become of it. They

style themselves practical; they make two smoke-
stacks smoke where none had smoked before. They
succeed—as it is called.

Few, it should be said, are single-minded in their
adoption of this program. Men leave the world of
illusions as Lot's wife left her native city, unable to
keep from looking back. There are those who had
been taught to believe that if you had two loaves of
bread, you sold one, and bought white hyacinth for
your soul. If they now part with white hyacinth to
increase their stock of bread, it is with a proviso.
Many hope to go in for a different ideal by and by.
They want material goods first, sometimes because
they believe that in this way they "can do more good
in the end," more often because they believe in
"safety first." Others, who do not delude themselves that they will reject late in their career a
scheme of life they have followed from the beginning, preserve a degree of loyalty to non-possessive
ideals as they go along. They periodically donate
a tithe of their accumulating possessions to causes
they believe to be worthy. Then, too, many an apparently unmixed desire to possess reaches beyond
itself and is colored by fusion with other impulses,
such as the desire to give pleasure to loved ones or
the desire to exercise power. Now while the desire
to possess for others is still a desire to possess, this

does not eliminate the "for others," just as the definition of love which makes it "selfishness for two," does not succeed in making it identical with selfishness for one. The same is true of the desire for possessions as a means to the exercise of power. The possessive element is there, but in an imaginative setting very different from that where the thing ultimately aimed at is social recognition, economic security, or the opportunity of enjoyment which money assures. The possessive idealists, then, are not people of one unqualified desire. Indeed, in the case of many whose chief business is the enlargement of possessions, the creative element is of such significance that we may think of them as double-personalities, and may speak of them after the manner of Francis Thompson's ode to Cecil Rhodes:

> They that mis-said
> This man yet living, praise him dead.
> And I too praise, yet not the baser things
> Wherewith the market and the tavern rings.
> Not that high things for gold,
> He held, were bought and sold,
> That statecraft's means approved are by the end;
> Not for all which commands
> The loud world's clapping hands,
> To which cheap press and cheaper patriots bend;
> But for the dreams,
> For those impossible gleams

He half made possible; for that he was
Visioner of vision in a most sordid day:
This draws
Back to me Song long alien and astray.

All of which is to say that the thick-skinned individual who aims no further than to take all he can
get, and to keep all that he is not forced to give up,
is the exception. And it is not the exception but the
rule that determines quality. Still, while it is true
and important that those whose chief desire is to
possess do not constitute one homogeneous type, and
that their attitude toward life may not be characterized as undivided allegiance to material goods, it is
just as true and important that the desire for economic power is for all of them the central desire.
Whatever other ideals they may endeavor to con-
serve, this particular end they aggressively pursue.
Whatever they may do or leave undone, the underlying purpose of life, always more or less consciously
active, is that the increasing years shall show a net
gain in what the bank will accept as collateral and an
extension of control over men and things. And they
smile indulgently, condescendingly, or sneeringly,
as the case may be, at the suggestion of any other
philosophy. Their theory is that "you've got to accept conditions as they are"; that "business is busi-

ness"; and they have a slogan: "Nothing succeeds like success."

Not so the others. They adopt a program radically different. On the mountain top they too came face to face with disillusion, and the outlook of youth, like a garment of happy memories, was laid away forever. But they saw what the others failed to see —the vision of a world transformed. It is this they seek. Many soon forget the vision, give up the venture, and join the majority. Some become wanderers, spiritual knights of the road, refusing the responsibility of the search. Others, losing heart, transfer the goal of their endeavor to a compensatory world to come. A few, however, hear a voice in the night, saying, "In vain do men seek to find that which exists nowhere but in their dreams. The world of your vision is not found, but created." And a few of the few accept the challenge.

So the minority want to help create a new world, not to possess the old one. Often uncertain and in disagreement as to the kind of world the new one should be; not always able to suggest a feasible way to the realization of their goal; they are clear, and at one, that existing social and political ideals must become quite different if life on earth is to be either happy or noble. Their position is easily misunder-

stood and still more easily misrepresented. There is
the charge, for example, that those who aim at changing the conditions of life are actuated by envy and
malice rather than by the hope of a better world;
that what they really want is a redistribution of possessions in their favor. It is not an easy charge to
meet, and for several reasons. In the first place,
some of those who are loudest in their denunciation
of existent conditions *are* interested primarily in
what they shall eat and wherewithal they shall be
clothed. They belong with the majority, whose
ideals are possessive; sometimes, indeed, they illustrate greed in its very worst form. Then, too, no
matter how radical and sincere a man's renunciation
of possessions may be, he cannot disregard them altogether. If he is to change the world, he must remain alive in it, and thus, unless he belongs to the
few who escape the problem through inheritance or
marriage, or to whom the gods have granted a unique
courage, he must pay some attention to the acquisition of material goods. Besides, to be effective he
must acquire some measure of power in the form of
influence or machinery. And as things are now, the
attainment of either is very difficult for those whose
intellectual and moral qualities are unsupported by
material resources. Consequently, those who aim at
a new heaven and a new earth cannot be expected to

be indifferent to possessions. They must make a living, and they must make more, or remain socially
ineffective. Nor is this the last word. The man who
aims to change the world is no more a person of one
desire than the man whose chief concern is ownership. Just as the interests of the latter reach beyond
his central purpose, so do those of the former. One
of the interests which thus normally lives side by
side with the desire for social change is the interest in
possessions.

The point is worth a little more fundamental consideration. Bertrand Russell, in his *Principles of
Social Reconstruction*, one of the big and living books
called forth by the war, makes this statement:
"When we are fed and clothed and housed, further
material goods are needed only for ostentation." In
the first English edition of the work, and in the
American edition, which for some reason was published under the title *Why Men Fight*, a footnote
adds this qualification, almost as an afterthought:
"Except by that small minority who are capable of
artistic enjoyment." Innocent as the footnote appears, it gives the case away. It suggests that the
needs of some men are not limited to being fed and
clothed and housed. Granted, for the sake of argument, that the footnote is correct in limiting those
other needs to a certain small minority, is it not a

fact that we are supposed to be endeavoring to make
them the needs of more and more, and that in so far
as we succeed we call it progress?   Moreover, what *is*
it to be fed and clothed and housed?   The Eskimo
is fed and clothed and housed; so is the Australian
savage, after his fashion.   Are their standards satisfactory?

Few people, in the nations called civilized, would
say so, even if many of them are themselves most
miserably situated.   The reason is, of course, that one
of the more obvious marks of advance in civilization
is just the development of discrimination in food and
clothing and shelter.   As Georg Simmel has suggested, the very concept of value, and thus the beginning of a cultural stage of life, has its origin in man's
preference for one object, rather than for another,
as the means of satisfying elemental wants.   So long
as hunger is satisfied by anything that can be chewed
and digested, so long as the choice of clothing constitutes no problem, and the question of housing is
nothing more serious than finding a sheltered place
to lie down in, the human level has hardly been
reached.   If, however, it is not a matter of *mere*
food and clothing and shelter but also *kind* of food
and clothing and shelter, is this not another way of
saying that, up to a certain point at least, the impulse
to possess is essential to the enrichment of life?   One

therefore wishes that Mr. Russell, in revising his book, had developed the implications of the footnote. He would have done it with the objectivity of thought, the power of discrimination, and the clarity of style which are his in such rare measure. He could have shown, as few others, that poverty imprisons the spirit, and that therefore the vow of poverty does not represent a desirable ideal even if it were shown to be a feasible one. He might then have indicated concretely how the desire for ownership may play its part in the realization of the richest total of satisfaction for all. Instead of this, he dropped the footnote altogether, and in its place added (to the previous statement, "When we are fed and clothed and housed, further material goods are needed only for ostentation") the words, "or to gratify the greed of possession, which, though instinctive, and perhaps partly ineradicable, is not admirable." In these sweeping words Mr. Russell erases all moral distinction based upon kinds or degrees of acquisitiveness. And the doctrine which he in this way deliberately and unreservedly enunciates is more or less consistently applied by most of us to the social idealism of others. That is why it is easy to fall into the error under consideration, the error of mistaking the spirit of reform for greed in disguise.

The whole difficulty grows out of a false psychol-

ogy. Human impulses are assumed to run along on
independent tracks like trains out of a central station
—one headed for possessions, another for this or that
pleasure, a third for esthetic satisfaction, and so on.
The truth is, however, that impulses are abstractions; the reality is a person. And whatever else
person means, it means some sort of organic whole in
which desires are related to one another as color and
shape are related in the case of objects. When a
man's attitude changes with regard to possessions it
does not leave unaffected his concern for those he
loves, his interest in public welfare, his enjoyment
of beauty. What takes place is a reorganization of
desires, with a more or less pronounced shift of emphasis. The man, then, who aims at changes in social
structure is not one who is without an interest in
property, but one in whom this interest bears a certain relation to other interests. Nor is he necessarily
a man who pays little attention to property. Indeed,
under certain circumstances—when, for example, a
given state of society (as the present one) rests upon
a distribution of material goods which makes a happy
life impossible for the mass of men—his proposed
reforms may have most direct reference to a change
in the status of possessions.

There are thus psychological and sociological reasons why the interest in possessions may have a place

in the lives of those who object to the world as ¦
But this makes it natural, under present conditi___,
to misunderstand them and easy to misinterpret them.
Nevertheless, it does not require extraordinary intellectual penetration nor unattainable freedom from
prejudice to discover individuals about us whose abili-
ties and energies are dedicated to the realization of
a more worthy social state. They do not talk about
accepting life on the terms offered; they propose to
bargain with life for the best terms obtainable for
mankind. Their theory is that things should conform to men, rather than men to things, and they
too have a slogan: "The things that are seen are temporal." They are found among all peoples, in all
classes, are of both sexes, with and without schooling,
agnostics and believers; and relatively few as they
number, were they suddenly to despair and join the
majority, a great winter would settle down upon the
spirit of mankind.

There comes a time, then, when a man adopts, or,
rather, when he may be said to have adopted, one or
the other of these two programs as the central interest of life. And we must hold fast to the fact that
each program represents a form of idealism. We
are not in the habit of applying the term idealist to
the man whose chief thought is of increasing possessions. He is the practical man, who builds on a solid

foundation of reality. It is the man who aims to transform the world, usually without considering conditions, whom we call idealistic. But this is mere usage. This usage has its justification indeed in a vital difference between the two, but what this difference consists in is not apprehended, and so we confuse a most important issue. The difference between the two is not that one espouses ideals and the other does not. The difference is in the kind of ideal espoused. In the most important sense of the term all men are idealists. All men make sacrifices for chosen ends. All men act on the hypothesis that ideas are realizable in the form of concrete goods. All men give their allegiance to plans that can come to fruition only if events can be made to conspire. All men believe in the imaginative inauguration in the present, of campaigns for the conquest of the future.

Those who scoff at the idealists are of the same genus but of another species. Their ridicule does not prove that they are on a more solid basis themselves, but only that they have no use for a specific type of idealism. Sometimes, it is true, they are opposed to a specific idealism because they are persuaded that it makes so little contact with actual conditions as to be quite impossible of realization. But at other times they are opposed to it just because they fear

that it *is* realizable, and because they know, or half
consciously suspect, its bearing upon their own
schemes. In other words, the conflict between the
so-called idealists and the so-called practical men is a
conflict of ideals. And since it is the very nature of
ideals to become transmuted into realities and thus
to alter the conditions of life, an unclouded appreciation of this fact is of utmost social significance.
Such clarification concentrates attention where it belongs, upon the aims and ambitions of men, and the
bearing of these upon the common life of all. I do
not mean to minimize the profound difference between these two types of idealists, but only to deny
the fictitious claim of the so-called practical man that
his projects are the more "real."

The error just considered gives rise to a second,
namely, that possessive idealism is the only form of
idealism in harmony with the conditions of life, and
that the possessive idealist, accepting life on the terms
offered, does not undertake the hopeless task of trying to change the world, but makes the best of it as
it is. Now in an important sense this is clearly not
the case. In point of fact, who consumes more energy than the possessive idealist in trying to change
the world? The physical features of the earth, the
territorial divisions of it, the political, social, and
economic organizations under which men live, their

institutions of learning, their clubs, their churches,—
in a word, *everything*—is constantly being molded
and fashioned by those who announce it as the quin-
tessence of wisdom that "you've got to accept conditions as they are." Every community the world
round is in a continuous process of adjustment and
readjustment in response to the refusal of the great
army of the possessive idealists to be satisfied with
things as they are. And when we turn to their leaders, what more colossal dreamers have there been
than the so-called men of practical affairs—warriors,
rulers, diplomats, captains of industry? By the great
possessive idealists no scheme is thought too vast, too
costly, too hazardous, too Utopian, if it gives promise
of changing the world in the direction of the approved ideal. To this end they long ago converted
a nomadic society into an agricultural, and later an
agricultural into an industrial. To the same end they
continue to construct highways, span rivers, drive the
iron steed on land, push ships across the sea, build
cities and states. Accept conditions? Why, the desire to change conditions is the very breath of their
nostrils.

The truth is that no man accepts conditions as they
are. It was once reported to Carlyle that Margaret
Fuller had said, "I accept the universe"; and Carlyle, with his usual sweetness remarked, "Gad, she'd

better." Yet neither Margaret Fuller nor Carlyle actually accepted the universe, nor does any human being accept the universe; and Gad, he'd better not. For to project one's self into a future different from the present, to think of one's self as there doing deeds or enjoying goods of one sort or another, and to try to order the present in furtherance of a future thus conceived, is the essential difference between the human and the brute mind. That is to say, all men are busy, some more, some less, trying to realize ideals. They may not be *ideal* ideals; that is, they may not be what some moral or religious or other standard would require; but they are ends for which other ends are sacrificed, which is the essence of an ideal. And when a man ridicules another for being too idealistic, he does so on the tacit assumption that his own ideal is standard.

Now it is obvious that we live in a time which places property above all other considerations. Our industrial organizations, our political and social institutions, our press, churches, educational systems, the forces of respectability equally with the forces of labor, all coöperate to emphasize property ideals. Interest in improving the conditions of life are not entirely wanting; indeed, in some forms it is widely prevalent and in some instances very strong; still, in the vast majority of people it is strictly subservient to the acquisition of economic power. But who can avoid the suspicion that our program is ruinous? Wealth incalculable has been swept away and a heavy mortgage has been placed upon the future. Nine million lives and irrecoverable treasures of genius have been offered up, and our whole outlook has been poisoned with hate. Nor was this a stroke of fate that came upon us from without. The war was the ripened fruit of a long culture. It magnified what was true before it began, and is true still. Every city and hamlet tells the same story. There is something profoundly wrong with our philosophy. We are betrayed by a deceptive ideal, since what we call society is our idealism in action. Therefore the choice before us is clear: a new idealism or ruin. There seems to be no escaping the conclusion that our present philosophy of life is leading us to destruction. Unless we do away with it, it will do away with us. The minority idealists are right; the world must be re-made.

At this point we are sure to be solemnly told that to remake the world is not a simple matter. And it is not. To discover defects in our social system is easy enough, much easier than to give conceptual form to a better one or to suggest how a better one may be arrived at. On the other hand the cause is a supreme one. The stake is stupendous and it is

not demonstrated that the difficulties cannot be met.
Nor is the way of procedure utterly dark.

One step is clearly indicated. We must divest ourselves of our theological conception of human nature. In spite of our outward scorn of theology, most
of us are at heart disciples of Augustine or Calvin.
We believe in original sin and predestination. We
no longer employ the old terminology, and that is
the extent of our reform. We continue to think of
human nature as essentially base and essentially unchangeable. Mr. Burleson was speaking for many
another in his reported interview. "No man," he is
quoted as saying, "has any more sympathy than I
have for the poor fellow bent over working with a
pick for $1.50 a day. I'll do all I can to lighten
that man's burden. But," he added, "do you know
why that man can't make more money? It's up
here," and he pointed to his forehead. "It's the
shape of his brain. It's fatality. God Almighty
did that, and you can't change it. You're challeng-
ing Providence. Distribute all the wealth in the
country with absolute equality, and what would happen within a year? It would all be back in the same
hands."

There it is: the damnation of the many without
remedy, the election of the few to favor, and the
helplessness of all to change the decree. The most

noticeable difference between the Calvinistic and the Burlesonian theology is that in the former God does business on a credit basis, while in the latter he pays cash as he goes.

Moreover, the people who escape this theology are exposed to other influences which distort their conception of human nature. The greater part of a man's life, as Gilbert Murray has said, "is rigidly confined in the round of things that happen from hour to hour. It is exposed for circumstances to beat upon; its stream of consciousness channeled and directed by the events and environments of the moment." And there is enough, and more than enough, in the circumstances that beat upon a man's life from hour to hour, to convince him of human greed, as there is little enough, from this limited view, to encourage a belief in human improvableness. This is notoriously true of business and industry, and even if not notorious is true of the professions. Indeed, even those who rise above their immediate environment and attain to some appreciation of human life in its historical aspect are by no means certain to escape. By many such emancipated souls progress is regarded as illusory.

Unquestionably, a most profound and comprehensive demonstration of human achievement was placed before us when it was shown that man has not

crawled down from a being that was almost a god,
but has struggled up from a creature that was not
even an ape.   Nevertheless, what has been the effect
of the doctrine of Evolution upon our belief in man's
inherent depravity and unchangeableness?   The writers who, on the strength of Evolution, have placed
a higher estimate upon human nature, or have put
a more hopeful interpretation upon man's destiny,
may be counted on the fingers of one hand: John
Fiske, Henry Drummond, Lafcadio Hearn, Mrs.
Annie Besant—there are not many others.   And
these are not generally thought to have made out a
case.   By the majority, the discovery of warfare as
the law of animal survival has been accepted as a
justification of its adoption as a rule of conduct
among men.   "Survival of the Fittest," which for
Darwin and Spencer and Huxley meant the survival
of those that *could* survive, has, in spite of their express warning, been taken to mean the survival of
those that *should* survive.   Thus the great philosophic concept which is the peculiar contribution of
our time to the history of thought, and which deeply
colors our whole attitude toward life, instead of liberating us from the notion of the incurable depravity
of human nature, has assisted in its perpetuation.

Doubtless there is good reason why man finds it
so difficult to overcome this tragic idiosyncrasy, this

insistence upon his own baseness. It may be argued that it is the unconscious memory of those long ages when the human ancestor was brute among brutes, or that it is the testimony of man's own inner experience as of his outward observation. There is one factor, however, which such arguments leave out of account, and which undoubtedly has considerable to do with the production of human nature as it actually exhibits itself. This factor is the complexity of persons, institutions and things in response to which human beings develop. Of course everybody is aware of environment as a fact, but by no means everybody recognizes the nature of the rôle it plays. The general belief still is that human nature is something given and innate, and that the conditions of life result from the unfoldment or liberation of this something.

The error in this view has been keenly analyzed by John Dewey, especially in *Human Nature and Conduct*. Society always antedates the individual, and acts as a powerful force in the production of his "nature" out of his original equipment of impulsive capacity. Human nature is a double-barreled concept, pointing at inherent individual capacity and external social conditions. As long as we insist upon keeping the latter factor constant we can expect no radical change in the product. That people are acquisitive who develop to maturity in an acquisitive society does not prove them to be ruled by an innate acquisitive instinct. How far and how deep we can go in securing a different human nature by modifying the circumstances surrounding its development cannot be determined offhand, nor does it need to be. What does concern us is the fact that a different type of society would give us in the vast majority of people a very different kind of idealism than the dominant contemporary type.

The conception of such a society has been ably presented in an extraordinary little book by R. H. Tawney, and is aptly called by him the functional conception of society. "A society," he says, "which aimed at making the acquisition of wealth contingent upon the discharge of social obligations, which sought to proportion remuneration to service and denied it to those by whom no service was performed, which inquired first not what men possess but what they can make or create or achieve, might be called a Functional Society, because in such a society the main subject of social emphasis would be the performance of social functions."

Is such a reorganization of life feasible? Let us remember what is proposed. It is not proposed that we shake off the qualities of human nature as "dew drops from the lion's mane," nor that we build a

Utopia on purely imaginary foundation. The proposal amounts to a new orientation of life; an orientation that makes different use than is now done of the capacities of mankind. We all recognize that it is possible for an *individual* to organize his life around the desire to function rather than the desire to possess. Each of us is acquainted with people who successfully exemplify this principle even under present unfavorable conditions: teachers, preachers, artists of various kinds, those who find an outlet for this desire in business or industry, those who are devoted to the more remote goal of social reconstruction. The number of people in the world who put possessions second is large, even if it is small in proportion to those who do not. The proposed change would increase this number, until what is now the exception would be the rule. It would do this by making the desire to function an essential instead of an accidental feature of life.

So fundamental a change is not without its difficulties, and they are great difficulties, but there is no reason to regard them as insuperable. We are showing ourselves able to cope with our theological teachers; we may show ourselves able to cope with the class which is at present even more powerful—the business class. At present Business dominates the situation. But we are coming to believe that necessary functions of society should not be conducted without reference to the common good, and gradually the conception of what constitutes a necessary function of society is being enlarged to cover enterprises which were formerly permitted to go it alone. We may yet refuse to permit captains of industry to be the captains of our souls. Some people resent any movement in this direction as an attack on business. It is not an attack on business, but a defense of life.

The chief difficulty in the way of a functional society is the natural fear all classes of people feel that any disturbance of the acquisitive basis of society means economic insecurity. "As far as the mass of mankind are concerned," Mr. Tawney suggests, "the need which private property other than personal possessions does still often satisfy, though imperfectly and precariously, is the need for security. To the small investors, who are the majority of property-owners, though owning only an insignificant fraction of the property in existence, its meaning is simple. It is not wealth or power, or even leisure from work. It is safety. They work hard. They save a little money for old age, or sickness, or for their children. They invest it, and the interest stands between them and all that they dread most. . . . And this hunger for security is so imperious that those who suffer most from the abuses of property, as well as those

who, if they could profit by them, would be least inclined to do so, will tolerate and even defend them,
for fear lest the knife which trims dead matter should
cut into the quick." This economic security is a
fundamental need, but as Mr. Tawney points out,
"almost the gravest indictment of our civilization
is that the mass of mankind are without it." Judged
by its economic as well as its human fruits, acquisitive society is a palpable makeshift. We cannot admit it to be the final form of social organization.
The possessive ideal struts to-day as never before.
But to-morrow is another day, and in it we may look
for the triumph of a better ideal.

CHAPTER III

RIGHT FOR RIGHT'S SAKE

"Two things," according to Kant's familiar remark, "fill the spirit with ever new and increasing wonder and awe the more reflection busies itself therewith: the starry heavens above and the moral law within." Seneca spoke to the same effect: "To whatever country we are banished, two things go with us: our part in the starry heavens above and the world around, and our sole right in the moral instincts of our heart." It is not the mere fact that men feel under constraint to do certain things and refrain from doing others, which has excited admiration. It is the fact that, however various the specific things demanded in different places and at different times, they are all done under the sense of their rightness. The more pure this feeling the higher the moral quality of the act has been thought to be. To do right in the hope of a reward, from fear of punishment, or as a means to happiness has generally been regarded as selfishness, none the better for being enlightened or long-headed selfishness. Few people have responded enthusiastically to

Paley's dictum: "Virtue is the doing good to mankind, in obedience to the will of God, and for the
sake of everlasting happiness"; and Mill has himself told us that his Utilitarianism, which made the
Greatest Happiness Principle the foundation of
morals, excited in many minds, and among them
some of the most estimable in feeling and purpose,
an inveterate dislike. They designated the theory
"as utterly mean and groveling; as a doctrine worthy
only of swine." The majority of people, who have
not bothered their heads about the matter, were they
to examine their feelings, would find that they spontaneously refuse to call an act moral if it is done in
consideration of ulterior ends. Such acts may be
expedient or proper; but to be moral an act must be
done because it is right. In short, we may say that
by fairly general consent the highest concept the
mind of man has attained to is the concept of right
for right's sake.

This view is set forth by A. Clutton-Brock in an
earnest, straightforward little book called *The Ultimate Belief*. The great need of the times, he argues, is a philosophy which supplies some underlying reason why men are to do the things that need
to be done. And there is a philosophy to which any
unperverted mind responds, and which will redeem
our distracted and broken age. People will not do

without reasons. If they fail to get good ones, they will get bad ones. Some sort they will have. And the sort they now get, he thinks, is generally bad, because they bear no relation to anything good in itself. What we need to learn is that everything we do should be done for the sake of certain absolutely ideal ends, ends which, in distinction from all others, are sought for their own sakes. Our superficial and ruinous hand-to-mouth utilitarianism must be replaced by a philosophy of the spirit. The multiplicity of our material desires, now so imperious, must be made subservient to the desires of the spirit.

Now the philosophy of the spirit tells us that "the spirit desires three things and desires these for their own sake and not for any further aim beyond them. It desires to do what is right for the sake of doing what is right; to know the truth for the sake of knowing the truth; and it has a third desire which is not so easily stated, but which I will now call the desire for beauty." "These three desires," he continues, "and these alone, are the desires of the spirit; and they differ from all our other desires in that they are to be pursued for their own sake, and can, indeed, only be pursued for their own sake. If they are pursued for some ulterior end, they change their nature. . . . So the spirit has three activities, and three alone, as it has three desires; namely, the moral, the intellectual, and the esthetic. And man lives so that he may exercise these three activities of the spirit, and for no other reason." All other theories of life make the business of living primary, and these higher values subsidiary. "But the philosophy of the spirit says that the business of living is subsidiary to them, and that man can only satisfy himself in his life if he lives so that he may exercise the activities of the spirit and not so that he may go on living."

There are some people whom this type of reasoning leaves utterly cold, and others in whom it stirs up nothing but antipathy. Most men and women, however, who have thought seriously about our chaotic moral and spiritual situation find in it something reassuring and appealing, and they are predisposed to minimize, if not quite to overlook, a defect in the theory which it is very costly to disregard. What life demands of us—has always demanded and demands especially just now—is intelligent choice between concrete, relative values or goods. Shall we be for prohibition or against it; shall we vote for Republicans, Democrats, or a Third Party; shall we stay in the church with our doubts or get out and let our aspirations take their chances in isolation; shall we approve of this design for the high school, this picture for our home, this gift for a friend, or some other? Such are the options constantly presented to us, and it is with reference to them that we need light. We are not called upon to be loyal to goodness or truth or beauty *as such,* but always to *some specific case* of the good, the true, the beautiful. And the defect of the theory in question is that in its anxiety to emphasize the need of *loyalty* to goodness, truth, and beauty, it leaves the *concrete object* of that loyalty to be determined by chance. Whether it entails this result logically or not (a question which would require a separate chapter to discuss) it does so practically.

Perhaps the best way to satisfy ourselves on this head is to study an example of the theory in action on a scale which makes its features clearly recognizable. And none will better serve this purpose than the relation of the German militarists to Kant's doctrine of duty, if we can divest ourselves of the predisposition to see in it something peculiarly German. For we have here an excellent example of how the doctrine of right for right's sake, enunciated by one of the noblest spirits of all time, lent itself naturally and inevitably to exploitation by men who were interested certainly chiefly, if not entirely, in economic and political, rather than moral ends.

In Kant's view there are two distinct kinds of obligations which all men feel. We know we ought to

do certain things because we desire certain consequences, and we know we ought to do other things
regardless of consequences. We say, for example,
"I ought to put aside some money, for I'd hate to be
dependent when I'm old, like so and so." That is,
the obligation is not absolute, but conditional; it is
incurred only because we have previously adopted a
program which implies it. But there is also an
unconditional obligation, as the obligation to tell the
truth. Men know that they ought to tell the truth,
not because it pays, but because it is their duty. And
this unconditional obligation to act from a sense of
duty regardless of consequences is Kant's famous
categorical imperative. This is the real ought, the
other is a pseudo-ought. This is the ought in truth,
the other an ought in word only.

Now Kant was perfectly convinced that all men
acknowledge themselves to be under obligation in
this unconditional manner. Indeed, the monitor in
the human breast called conscience was for him, as
we know, one of the two transcendent wonders of the
world we live in. And from this fact—the universality and finality of conscience, as voiced in the categorical imperative—he makes some most interesting
and, alas, tragic deductions.

For one thing, if men recognize an obligation to
act from a sense of duty, and duty alone, this proves

that morality is other-worldly in its origin and nature. How does it show that? Because nothing in the world of nature can account for the conviction. From the world of nature we can learn what is, what has been, and what is to be, but never what ought to be. Take natural science. From the observation of natural phenomena (Kant would say) we may learn that the kernel of the white oak acorn tastes sweet while that of the red oak tastes bitter; that three million years ago the horse was hardly bigger than a good-sized cat, with five toes on each foot, instead of one; that thirteen thousand years from now our north pole will point to big blue Vega, instead of to Polaris, and that then it will be much colder on earth in winter and much warmer in summer than now. But no amount of investigation could ever lead to the discovery that the white oak's behavior is more ideal than the red oak's; that it really wasn't right for the horse to lose most of its toes; or that it is immoral for Vega to supplant Polaris. Morality has nothing to do with nature, and so cannot be discovered there.

What nonsense! you say. Naturally no trace of moral quality can be discovered through the study of things; but what about the study of people and society? No, Kant would reply; there is no help in that direction either. History, sociology, psychology, are as helpless in this matter as physics or astronomy. Of course, if the sense of duty were a mere subjective feeling, it might be accounted for, say, by psychology, or physiology. In that case, however, it would no longer be duty, but a name for the way Tom, Dick, or Harry feel; and duty, when it ceased to be felt, would cease to be. Which is exactly what men will not admit. A man's duty is a man's duty, whether he acknowledges it or not. Or if the sense of duty were the feeling of social pressure, it might be accounted for, say, by the conditions under which men live. But this again is impossible. The conditions under which men live do indeed make certain lines of conduct seem advisable, expedient, wise, or the reverse, but they cannot make them moral or immoral. And this, Kant holds, is clear from the fact that any obligation arising out of the exigencies of life is a conditional obligation—one that may be confronted with the question: Why ought that to be done?

Take the person who says: "I ought to be putting aside some money for a rainy day." Obviously he is obliged to do this only if he objects to becoming dependent upon others. And if when asked why he should not become dependent upon others, he replies, "Because that would be shifting to other shoulders burdens which are properly mine," that is not a final answer. He may be asked, "Why not?" And so on without end. Nowhere in the world of concrete life do we reach an act, or an object, or a person, or an institution which commands by inherent right. It is always a derived or borrowed right. The obligations imposed by the exigencies of life are all conditional obligations. Well, then, since the study of nature yields only facts but *no* obligations, and since the study of society accounts for *conditional* obligations only, there is either no *categorical* imperative at all, or it has a source other than the world of sense. But categorical imperative there indubitably is. Hence, the law of morality is the law of a world above nature.

Now this super-mundane origin and nature of moral obligation draws after it consequences of the most far-reaching significance. From it Kant's inexorable logic deduces the conclusion that the criterion or test of moral conduct can have no reference to objects or interests of every-day life. If the categorical imperative is by birth and allegiance otherworldly, so is its mother-tongue. And in this case there can be no transfer of allegiance and no learning of a new language. Kant was assured, as many people still are, that if the moral standard loses its other-worldly reference, it ceases to be moral, whatever else it may be. That other world, however, is not a material world, but a world of reason; not a world of things, but a world of forms, types, principles. Therefore a test of morality which reflects that world must be a pure principle of reason, a rule of conduct unaffected by the objects or acts through which it gets realization. As logical validity is solely a question of conformity to certain rules of procedure, and not at all a question of what the argument is about, so moral validity is agreement with a certain formula, and has no reference whatever to the conditions under which the formula is applied. Morality has to do with the soul of conduct, not with its body, to say nothing of the clothes it may temporarily put on.

Kant deploys all his immense resources of learning, of logic, and of exposition to enforce this idea. He cannot reiterate it enough. There is but one thing in the universe, he insists, which has absolute value, value in and of itself. Everything else is only relatively good. And this one supreme good is a disposition or will that looks with proud disdain upon human inclinations and desires, that holds itself aloof from all considerations of human weal or woe, and is inspired solely by reverence for duty. Granted that such purity of will is unattainable on earth, or if attained, cannot be maintained. Nevertheless, it is enjoined as an ideal upon every rational being.

And in the surrender to this ideal man realizes the highest spiritual achievement possible on earth, and does the only thing a man can do which is justly deserving of praise.

This is not all that Kant said about morality, but we need not attempt a fuller statement of his moral theory since our problem has to do with his doctrine of duty for duty's sake and certain fortunes of that doctrine when applied. And who will deny that there is something noble and sublime about this doctrine? Whom do we detest more than the man who does right for what he thinks to get out of it, and who are the great heroes and heroines of history but the men and women who, as we say, did right for right's sake, not counting the cost?

A noble doctrine, but as dangerous as it is noble. And for this reason: However purely formal we may make duty by definition, duty as we meet it face to face in actual life is always embodied in conduct. And conduct means consequences. No matter how much a man may act without *regard* to consequences his actions will *have* consequences, and these consequences will have a bearing upon his life and the lives of others for good or ill. This being the case, what is the social effect of the doctrine that man realizes his highest self when he turns his back upon consequences and reverently follows duty for duty's sake?

Well, for one thing, it means the substitution of a blindfolded morality for a morality with eyes; and for another, which is the inevitable corollary of the first, the surrender of man's best impulses into the hands of those who have the intelligence, the power, and the will to define the duty and to exploit those impulses for their own ends.

This is very clear in the way the philosophers of militarism made use of this philosophy. They seized and exploited the opportunity which the doctrine offered them. Nothing could be better adapted to their need than the prevalence among the people of a sense of duty which asks no questions. That is why the philosophers of militarism dwell upon the sacredness of the categorical imperative, and then go on to show that militaristic imperialism is its visible embodiment, for which therefore, as for a good beyond price, every individual must sacrifice all he holds dear.

Take Treitschke. Nothing could be wider apart than the political and national ideals of Kant and Treitschke. For Kant the future organization of nations is a fraternity of republics engaged in friendly rivalry to work out man's great destiny on earth. This, in Treitschke's view, is a perfectly meaningless abstraction. He lost his temper whenever he referred to it. To him the be-all and the end-all of the state is power, and "he who is not man enough to look this fact in the face," he said, "should not meddle in politics." Nevertheless, when it comes to showing that this is not only "in the nature of things," but in the nature of duty; that might is also right (a doctrine which men do not find it easy to accept), what does he do? He falls back upon Kant; and by the use of a kind of logical magic he identifies national honor with the categorical imperative. National honor is the "sublime moral good" which has something about it "in the nature of unconditional sanctity," and which thus "compels the individual to sacrifice himself for it." That is why the thought of war lifts up his soul. That is why he is sure that "God will see to it that war always recurs as a drastic medicine for the human race." For war, don't you see, horrible, gruesome war, is the categorical imperative in uniform.

This exploitation of a people's idealism, evident enough in Treitschke, is transparently clear in Bernhardi's widely read volume, *Germany and the Next War*. Bernhardi, a cavalry general, and writer of books on technical military subjects, is a disciple of Treitschke, and his philosophy is that of his master. But he presents it in an elaborated, popularized, and contemporary form, thus leaving less to be inferred. It is well known that the whole book is a pæan of

war as the God-given means to the realization of
German supremacy. Nothing can be more open or
frank than Bernhardi's declaration of the intrinsic
superiority of German civilization, or more straightforward than his insistence upon not only the right,
but the duty of Germany to impress her civilization
upon the world. The argument, however, with which
he backs up this view is by no means so familiar.
Quite naturally, too. Men are not inclined to spend
time examining an argument intended as a proof of
their moral and intellectual inferiority. It is an
argument, nevertheless, with which it is important
that we acquaint ourselves thoroughly, for only by
so doing can we at all appreciate the subtlety and
the strength of this philosophy as we ourselves
hold it.

The great law of life, says Bernhardi, is struggle;
"supplant or be supplanted," as Goethe put it. Between individuals or groups within a nation, this
struggle is restrained and regulated in the interest
of social welfare, because behind individuals and
groups "stands the State, armed with power, which
it employs, and rightly, not merely to protect, but
actively to promote, the moral and spiritual interests
of society." The situation, however, is quite different as regards the relation between States. For
"there is no impartial power that stands above the

rivalry of States, to restrain injustice, and to use that rivalry with conscious purpose to promote the highest ends of mankind." Consequently, on this larger stage things must be allowed to take their course; "each people must play its own part and promote its own ends and ideals." And this again is in the very nature of things. Between nations any "dispute as to what is right is decided by the arbitrament of war." "Any action in favor of collective humanity outside the limits of the State and nationality is impossible."

Nor is it merely impossible; it is also immoral. Immoral? Yes, immoral. Because in lunging on over the prostrate bodies of other peoples, jaws set, dripping sword in hand, the aggressive State not only gives expression to an irresistible biological law which listens to no logic and responds to no appeal. It does that, but it does more. It realizes the high spiritual end for which it and indeed the world exist—"the moral education of the human race." When we fix our eyes upon "the idealism of the main result," Bernhardi assures us, "the brutal incidents inseparable from every war vanish completely," and we see in the relentlessly aggressive State an object of supreme moral grandeur.

Bernhardi's reasoning is as simple as it is startling. The state which knows no law but power is made moral through the fact that it compels its people to be moral. For what is true morality but blind renunciation of all personal interests for the sake of duty? In any other kind of state men will be petty and selfish. The French, for example, have their doctrine of natural rights, the English their theory of utility, while the Americans demand a return in cold cash. With all of them it is a question of driving a good bargain. Thus they are materialists, time-servers, one and all. And the reason is that the French, the English, and the Americans look upon the state as the servant of the people, not as their master. The German master-state, on the contrary, demands of its people unswerving loyalty to Kant's "gospel of moral duty." In Germany more than in any other state on earth (it is interesting that her only rival is Japan) life is organized upon this great principle. That is why the German state is the greatest moral institution on earth. And because in Germany it is not enough just to talk about the transitoriness of the goods of life, but their transitoriness must be deeply *experienced*, the German State, which demands this, is the earthly incarnation of the moral force at the heart of things, and the ambition of Imperial Germany is the temporal manifestation of the will of the eternal God. That is to say, washed in the blood of its people, redeemed by their sacrifice, the ruthless state is changed from monster to divinity.

All this shows, of course, the Kantian drift of Bernhardi's philosophy. And the more one reads him, the more central one discovers the categorical imperative to be. He urges reforms in popular education. Why? Not enough emphasis is put upon the gospel of duty. He finds fault with the church. Why? There is too much emphasis upon dogma, and not enough upon duty. He points out the imperative necessity of establishing a state-controlled press. Why? So that the "moral healthiness" of the nation may be safeguarded against "epidemics of ideas" which are subversive of the gospel of duty. For the same reason he issues a warning against the tendency to carry labor reforms to a point where work shall no longer be a moral discipline but a joyful exercise. Every change which makes for the physical vigor, and thus for the efficiency, of the toiler must be encouraged, but great care must be taken that work remains toil—that it is done from a sense of duty. It must never become a satisfaction in itself nor a means to other satisfactions. For only if work is done from a sense of duty, is it moral and does it forge men, which is the object of work. Even the factories and workshops must be temples to the gospel of duty.

That is why Prussia (the product of hard economic conditions) and not a fertile Rhine province, was divinely chosen for the great task of leading Germany up to the unrivaled conception of life which Kant taught her. And what Prussia has done and is yet to do for Germany, Germany has done and is yet to do for the world.

The same philosophy was voiced by Emperor William. Take for example a quotation from the newspaper report of the message sent by him to the vice-president of the Reichstag, following the opening of a drive on the western front. "The complete victory," he said, "fills me with gratitude. It permits us to live again one of those great moments in which we can reverently admire God's hand in history. . . . The heroic deeds of our troops, the successes of our great generals, and the wonderful achievements of those at home, have their roots in moral forces, and in the categorical imperative which has been inculcated in our people in a hard school."

It turns out, then, that Kant's noble theory is a book of checks, made out to bearer on demand, signed by the blind sense of duty, and good for whatever amount the holder may have the will to write in, and the power to collect. The militarists took possession of the checks, and they had the will to write in and the power to collect amounts which stagger the imagination. But the same thing took place in all countries. Nor is the practice limited to war times. So long as moral concepts pass current in abstract form they will be given the concrete value which the exigencies of the situation seem to require, even if the very purpose of morality is betrayed in the process. Nothing better could happen to us than that we should be cured of our sentimental infatuation for moral abstractions by being sent out to develop our moral constitutions in the air of actuality. As long as we refuse to do that, our daily lives will undermine and subvert the efforts we make periodically for life's ennobling.

We must therefore resist the appeal of formal morality, of the doctrine of right for right's sake, even when, as is sometimes the case, it is presented by men of lofty motives and has its roots deep in the hearts of mankind. We must free ourselves from this morality not because it is illogical or ignoble, but because it is a tragic mistake which inevitably leads to the selfish exploitation of the many by the few. Duty for duty's sake is a noble concept, but in practice it means blind obedience to a program outlined by some one else who is not so blind and may not be so noble. Right for right's sake is a noble concept, but concretely it turns out to be right for somebody's might's sake. Let it be recognized that there is no categorical and no formal imperative; that every duty is conditional and concrete; that morality must justify itself experimentally in terms of human welfare. Then aspiration will be linked with intelligence, heart with brains, the quest for the good life with the everyday business of living, and morality will serve the greatest cause mankind can be devoted to—the creation of a social order which shall encourage, rather than thwart, the development of the possibilities of human nature.

Morality thus conceived finds its incentive and its criterion where it finds its problems. It operates with and for, not merely upon, the inclinations and desires of men. For sacred abstractions it substitutes the sacredness of life. In place of making humanity a means to the realization of absolute ends, it aims at relative ends to further human interests. And while no one can say to what ultimate goal all these ends should bend and converge, nor, indeed, whether there is an ultimate goal, we can see far enough at least to assert with confidence that we want a nearer approach to a type of community where each shall have a realizable chance to make his life a satisfaction and a joy. Accordingly, the direction of promise is toward some conception of right which, instead of avoiding entanglement with the issues of life, finds its meaning and realization in and through them.

CHAPTER IV

MIGHT MAKES RIGHT

In sharp contrast with the view that the concept right shines by its own luster, and that moral rightness, as an aboriginal quality, is the standard to which all conduct should be directly or indirectly subservient, is the view that right is merely the reflected glow of successful action and wrong the shadow cast by defeat. That is to say, at the opposite pole from the theory that we should do right for right's sake is the theory that might makes right.

This thesis is not a new one. It was doubtless old in theory, as it certainly was in practice, when Thrasymachus of Chalcedon became its vigorous protagonist in Plato's *Republic*. But in more recent times the argument has acquired a new authority because it fits in with much else that we believe. There is first of all the general conviction that class war is an ineradicable feature of modern life. Then the wide acceptance of the Darwinian hypothesis, that survival is the symbol of fitness in the biological realm, has biased the modern mind in favor of the conception that moral ideas merely represent survival

in the field of conduct.   And the recent war gave
powerful endorsement to the same tendency.   We
were led to believe that in a national crisis moral
sentiments were more honored in the breach than in
the observance.   Victory seemed to depend upon laying aside a moral attitude slowly acquired, and sub-
stituting for it a more primitive, because a more
virile, war-like temper.   To be sure we were supposed to do this because it was right, but if any one
doubted, we did not *show* him that it was right; we
used *force*.   Not only so.   Leaders who appealed
to our sense of right and justice to win us to participation in the conflict appeared to lose interest in moral
considerations once victory was assured.   Some have
since gone so far as frankly to justify the exploitation of a people's moral convictions by those more
directly responsible for national success.   As a result
of these and other influences the doctrine that right
is whatever the stronger can force the weaker to accept has been lifted to a new level of cogency.   Ever
increasing numbers of aggressive people are disposed
to look upon conduct as a problem of what can be
"put across," while less aggressive spirits are tempted
to voice their disillusion in the words of Euripides:

O miserable virtue! thou art but a word,
And I have been following thee as a real thing!

The issue was therefore never so timely as at present. Accordingly, even those who repudiate the doctrine that right is only another name for might are under obligation to acquaint themselves with it. Not only because, as Mill says, "whoever is anxious that a discussion should go to the bottom of a subject, must rejoice to see the opposite side of the question worthily presented," but because of the temper of the times. If it ever was justifiable to deal superficially with morality it clearly is not so now. The mass of men can no longer be coerced by formal logic or frightened by divine revelation. Unless we are prepared to trust the outcome of the present determination to arrive at a new moral outlook to the elemental emotions of men and women, we shall need to face the situation frankly and fully. We shall need to back this question into a corner and demand an unambiguous answer. If morality is the last great superstition, if life is in reality and irremediably a regardless struggle for survival, let the brutal truth be public. The very sternness of the fact may redeem the situation. We will at least be on an honest basis. On the other hand, a morality of genuine authority, and life as something more than ill-disguised warfare may turn out to be intellectually defensible. In that case the gain will be great. A way will then have been found out of our present uncer-

tainty, not to say hypocrisy, and there will be no
further occasion for apologizing to our intellects
for the desire to live a good life. Intelligence,
indeed, will be recognized as indispensable to goodness.

The doctrine that might makes right rests upon
two main lines of argument, one negative, one positive, each historical in character. If we turn to history (it is claimed) we see moral standards rise and
fall. The history of ethics (or theory about the
moral life) has been largely that of attempts to discover and set forth some incontrovertible principle
to be used in the individual case to decide what is
moral and what immoral. The number of principles
to which this dignity has been ascribed is very great.
And it would seem to follow from this that no indu-
bitable criterion exists. Where so many principles
are put forward, each with a claim to supreme authority, but each opposed by equally sweeping counter-
claims of others, the natural conclusion would seem
to be that in point of fact authority is divided, that
there is no absolute standard, and that morality is
relative. This may be regarded as the negative line
of proof. Men have searched for an absolute moral
standard and have been unable to find one. But they
have been compelled to act. They have therefore
adopted such relative standards as the need for action

made necessary, and have called these the standards of right.

At this point the positive line of proof appears. Assuming that morality is relative, how are our present notions of right and wrong to be accounted for? How have actual conflicts between antagonistic moral ideals been resolved? The answer is, by warfare. The adjudication of differences between moral ideals is the result of a fight eventuating in the victory of one ideal over another. Where appearances point to the conclusion that a different method of settling conflicts was employed, this way of settlement had itself come to be accepted because of its victory in a previous contest.

For evidence we are once more referred to history. Take negro slavery in America. Here certain differences in political and economic practices gave rise to divergent ideals in North and South. How was the question of the rightness or wrongness of slavery settled? By force of arms. Might made right. Had the South vanquished the North, our moral ideas would have adjusted themselves to that outcome, and we would now believe slavery to be right. Any number of instances might be cited to point the same moral, but there is no need to multiply illustrations.

No one with a sense for actualities will deny that the argument has force. Especially in the contemporary world, replete with object lessons of the doctrine in application, numerous instances are ready to hand which show that, for all our moral phraseology, we do force people to adopt the mode of behavior we desire and to accustom themselves to thinking it right. In other words, there can be no question that might—the power to make an idea prevail by some means extraneous to the idea itself—is and has been an important factor in getting people to *believe* certain things right and certain things wrong. But has this *made* them right or wrong?   That is the question we must examine.

At the outset it is advisable to distinguish between two very different meanings. Might makes right may mean that what is right (according to some moral standard or other) must win its way against obstacles, and, being in itself powerless, must always rely upon might; or it may mean that in the struggle between competing interests of life, victory goes to the one having the backing of might, and that when we have become habituated to the interest which has thus become dominant we call this right.   It may mean that might is *essential to the triumph of right* or that right is *merely another name for the triumph of might*. And it is important to keep this distinction in mind because in the one case right retains a connotation of its own (whatever it may be), while in the other its meaning becomes synonymous with might, and thus loses any distinctive connotation.

Let us consider these two meanings in turn. And let us examine first the appeal to history to prove that the ideas of right and wrong, which are recognized as binding at any given time, have come to be so recognized through the exercise of might. We at once encounter a serious difficulty. How are we to determine just what history teaches? Nothing is more notorious than the prevalence of fundamental differences of causal interpretation among historical experts themselves. In so limited a field as United States history Channing finds New England the dominant factor, Turner the westward moving frontier, Beard the triumph of the property class, Bancroft the irresistible advance of divine purpose. Proving a proposition by generalizations from history is not like a demonstration in mathematics or an experiment in a laboratory. As clouds which are separate and distinct overhead become indistinguishable when they have drifted into a mass on the horizon, so the forces which played upon life as it was lived lose their individual identity when merged into the accumulated past. It is extremely difficult, if not impossible, to isolate specific causal factors and to determine the part they played in the general result. The complexity of life and the mortality of events force us to rest the case upon a few facts selected from the mass of more or less relevant data and thus to base our conclusion upon highly simplified evidence.

In this process of necessary simplification we are in constant danger of oversimplification, of failing to consider antecedents which really played a significant rôle. The argument from Negro slavery in America is in point. Let us admit, for the moment, that but for the Civil War slavery would still be regarded as right in America. We certainly cannot say that it was the victorious northern army (to use it as a symbol) which did the deed. It is generally agreed that the greatest single factor in bringing on the war was what in a blanket term we may call the abolition movement. It was this which kept irritating the South and kept stirring up uncompromising anti-slavery sentiment in the North until finally outraged feelings on both sides made a peaceful settlement of the issue impossible. It was this also which pushed the North through one crisis after another until victory was won.

Now the abolition movement was primarily the organized sense of the wrongness of negro slavery. Therefore if we do not get too far away from the intricacies of the actual conflict we cannot say that it was guns and soldiers, economic goods and geographical advantages which made slavery wrong; we must perforce include, perhaps even give the chief causal position to, the moral sentiment which brought these together and held them to their task. As well account for America's participation in the World War without counting in a deep yearning for world peace and a stubborn faith in Democracy, as to account for our present attitude towards slavery without referring to the moral convictions of those who engaged in the great struggle to eradicate it from American soil. And this would seem to show the presence of another agent besides might.

The adherents of the might makes right doctrine are not without a reply to this contention. They would say first of all, as already intimated, that this other factor, this sense of the wrongness of slavery, itself came to be accepted as the result of a previous fight. Were we to go back into history a little further we would again find a conflict of interests and an appeal to might, with victory going to the side that contended for the wrongness of slavery. And in the second place they would say that the word might must consequently not be taken in too restricted a sense. The weapons used at any given time are not all carnal. Many of the most powerful of them are of another temper, such as praise and blame and the whole round of moral terms. But the sophisticated person recognizes these as precipitates of former victories and as present weapons of warfare, means employed for the protection of one's own ideals and the annihilation of those of one's rivals. The sense of right and wrong may complicate matters, but it in no way invalidates the argument.

The first of these replies may be dismissed with a word, for it is in effect a begging of the question. Since the very point at issue is precisely whether our sentiments of right and wrong are in every case the product of an antecedent might, we cannot assume this to be true when confronted with a force which on the face of it appears to be an exception. The second reply, however, calls for more discussion. And there everything turns on how much we mean by the term might. If we use the word for all those forces, whatever they may be, which coöperate in bringing about a moral outlook, then might is indeed responsible for the moral ideals a people may from time to time espouse. But in that case the word has become symbol for so much that it has lost all distinctive meaning, and hence has lost the specific significance which gives and has given the might makes right doctrine its unique character among moral theories. To guard itself against attack it has surrendered its claim. For the force of reason is one thing, the force of arms another. To persuade some one to give up his ideal for yours or for a compromise-ideal in which both his and yours find partial realization, requires power, or, if one wishes so to speak, the exercise of might; but it is a power in which the ideal functions significantly, not a power external to the ideal which enforces its adoption willy nilly. And that makes all the difference in the world.

To neglect this fact is, as it seems to me, to read history too simply. I find it impossible to read history in such wise as to convince myself that the aspirational character of life, the capacity of men to envisage and to care for a wider and wider circle of ideals and more and more refined ideals, the gradual trend away from the appeal to mere might—that all this is the result solely or primarily of the strong, the clever, the regardless, to force their desires upon those not so gifted. There is something in the face of aspiring humanity which may not be left out of account, though impossible of nice definition and perhaps ultimately inexplicable. Undoubtedly a hint of it might have been detected in the eyes of our rudest ancestors, as sometimes its presence appears to be suggested in the behavior of our yet more backward relatives in the animal kingdom. It has flowered, as far as our knowledge goes, in what we call morality, in man's ability to imagine a fairer life than the immediately experienced one and in his skill gradually to translate the vision into fact. If anything is to be singled out, it is to this, in my judgment, rather than to physical strength or mental cleverness that moral progress is due.

Let us assume, however, that might has indeed dominated moral history. This is not the end of the story. We have merely discovered how moral concepts have arisen and fallen. History can do no more than tell us what, as a matter of fact, has characterized the morality of the past; it can give us no assurance that the same thing must characterize the morality of the future. But our problem is essentially a philosophical, not an historical one. We are endeavoring to discover whether it is the essential nature of right to reflect might. We thus return to the distinction between two meanings of might makes right. Granted that according to the historical record the morality of the past was dependent upon might, we are not on this account entitled to claim that this is the essential nature of right.

We must, therefore, turn to the other meaning of the phrase, which leads us to examine what morality is conceived to be by those who contend that might makes right. And we can say at least this much: it is absolutistic, and it is devoid of the quality ordinarily called moral. A little reflection should make this clear.

At first blush nothing appears more obvious than
the relativity of warfare morality. Not only is the
position that morality implies an immutable standard
attacked, but relative morality is avowed and defended. Yet what really happens is the substitution
of one form of absolutism for another. In place of
one immutable ethical truth we now have an indefinite number of impulses, aims, purposes, ideals, each
absolute in its own right. If they were relative to
some accepted scheme of life, if they were subservient to an end determined upon after a survey of the
situation in which the conflict arose, then an adjustment might be attempted in harmony with this
scheme or end. In that case we might agree to search
for a way to eliminate some desires, modify some,
and give free play to others, or we might seek to
discover a new goal in which the various conflicting
ends aimed at might each come to the largest realization possible under the circumstances. But this is
not the aim of warfare morality. Opposing ideals
are, as far as possible, to be counted out. The person who would hesitate to push his own claims regardless of others is disapproved of in favor of the
one who has no such scruples, on the ground that
there is no ideal to which other ideals may be called
upon to surrender their prerogatives. All ideals are
on the same footing. In other words, each desire

is absolute. That is why nothing remains but might to adjudicate between them.

And what of the moral character of the theory? The claim is that might makes *right*, yet if the implications of the position are followed up a little the word right gradually loses its meaning. The ablest advocate of the proposition on a national scale was Treitschke. He taught not only with frankness but with captivating enthusiasm that between nations there can be no right but might. The only consideration for a nation was how best to advance its own interests, regardless of the consequences to other nations. All intermediate means and ends were justified if they enhanced the national glory. Within a nation, on the other hand, might did not make right. There morality demanded the fullest possible coöperation of man with man and the most complete self-surrender to the common good. The foes of this double-standard morality have roundly denounced it as wily sophistry. It was not sophistry. It was at the worst a logical inconsistency. In the case of an individual or an organization of individuals, Treitschke believed in an absolute standard of right and wrong modeled after Kant's categorical imperative, which he admired almost as much as Kant himself did. In the case of nations, however, he was convinced that no such standard existed.

There was no super-nation, as there was a super-individual. Hence in the case of conflicts of interest between nations Treitschke could see no alternative but an appeal to force. But this amounted to saying (and the Treitschkian philosophy has long been so interpreted) that between nations there can be no question of right and wrong but only one of expediency and power. Now the warfare moralist properly sees no ground for applying the criterion to one set of ideals and not to another. Accordingly he applies to all conflicts of interests between man and man the doctrine that Treitschke applied to international conflicts only.

But does not the application of the doctrine in this thoroughgoing fashion abrogate morality altogether, just as its application to international situations abrogates morality in that field? Obviously the appeal to force can only show who is strong, not who is wrong, in the one case as in the other. To determine who is wrong some standard must be agreed upon which balances the ideals over against each other. Trying out the fighting qualities of those who champion the ideals is simply to turn one's back upon the merits of the case. Occasions may arise when, under existing conditions, human nature will not permit the conflict to be decided in any other way, but the question is whether this is to be regarded as a temporary

breakdown of the moral economy or its normal functioning. Warfare morality makes it the latter. Life
simply *is* a war of each against all and all against
each, and that is the end of the matter. And in such
a state the terms right and wrong, as Hobbes saw,
have no meaning. Under such conditions there is
but one commandment, however it may be glossed
over or refined:

> "Lay on, Macduff;
> And damn'd be him that first cries 'Hold, enough!' "

The logic of the doctrine pushes us a step further
than any statement of warfare morality which I have
seen contemplates. Conflicts between ideals are not
limited to the two spheres just considered. They
also take place within the life of the individual.
Each individual is himself the theater of conflicting
desires. And as we all know, some of life's deepest
tragedies grow out of this type of conflict. If might
makes right in the case of all other ideals, the same
formula must be applicable here. The development
of character is then no longer a problem in adjustment, but consists in satisfying the strongest impulse.
There may be an outcry at first, due to previous
habits of life, as in the case of other conflicts. Eventually, however, those aspects of the self which supported ideals that turned out to be doomed will

either be buried or will adapt themselves to the change. Thus in time personality will be shaped in conformity with the successively triumphant impulses, and the result must be regarded as morally right. Taken together with the outcome of the doctrine in the case of national and social relationships there is nothing left for the word moral to connote. In such a world a man's obligations may be summed up in the words of Royce: "Find your place, and farm it cleverly, for that is the whole duty of man."

That this is the consequence of what Huxley called "the gladiatorial theory of existence" would be obvious but for the interesting and significant fact that mankind believes morality to be something quite different. However vague the conception may be, however practice may fall short of profession, men and women acknowledge some sort of an ideal order superior in authority to things as they are. The language of every people is stocked with terms that reflect this faith. And this screens the warfare morality from being seen in its nakedness. Naturally the advocates of this philosophy drop into the common manner of speech, employing terms which disguise its real significance, which prevents the reader from appreciating the full consequence of the doctrine. Take the general admission that the weapons of moral warfare are not all carnal. In a theory which reduces moral terms to insidious means of gaining victory for one's ideals, what does the distinction amount to? A moral judgment is compelling just because it is believed to be a *moral* judgment, and not simply a blind under cover of which the moralizer aims to advance his own interests. By availing itself of the terminology of everyday speech, warfare morality induces a state of mind in the reader which has long been associated with this terminology, and so receives credit for being what it is not.

Or, take the use of the term "right." What is the meaning of this word in the phrase "might makes right"? In everyday speech, right has a specific connotation by virtue of its relation to an ideal order set over against nature. Possibly there is no justification for a moral philosophy of this kind. Yet it is beyond question that this much at least is what right means in the popular and even the cultivated mind. It is this which gives the word its peculiar significance in morality as distinguished, let us say, from its use in law or economics. In the warfare morality right can of course have no such meaning. "Might makes right" means in plain English, that there is no *right* at all; that what we call by that name is absolutely nothing more than a mode of behavior which the stronger, by virtue of his strength, has

been able to force upon the weaker. But by saying
"might makes *right*," rather than "right is a fiction,"
a quality is imported from a rival system which gives
the doctrine a moral aroma. Thus the illusion is
fostered that morality still lives. But the reader who
understands will not be deceived by this delicate odor
of sanctity. He will recognize it as the perfume of
a floral offering placed upon the bier of deceased
morality in memory of long association.

This leads to the heart of the problem. Warfare
moralists deserve credit for emphasizing the primal
right of human desires. Is the conclusion they draw
from this the only one logically to be drawn?
Clearly not, if morality is relative to men's purposes.
By whose compulsion must human life conform to
the rule of animal existence? We can decide to *make*
right and wrong mean something very different. The
way is suggested by what is expected to be done when
conflicts arise in the bosom of the individual. When
an individual is called upon to settle a conflict between his own ideals, he certainly does not ordinarily
let the various desires fight it out. There is often a
struggle, and sometimes a particular impulse does a
good deal of pushing and slugging, but, as a rule,
the individual aims at an adjustment in which the
various desires involved shall have consideration.
The pressure of the community, his own "larger"

good, a "remoter" good, any or all of these, and
other considerations still, may be brought in to check
the force of immediate desire. That is to say, intelligence enters to adjust the conflict in the interest
of a more comprehensive whole. This is accomplished through the creation of a new goal in which
the ideals in conflict have some sort of proportionate
representation. That is the unique function of intelligence in crises of this sort. We have already
extended the same method to conflicts between the
ideals of different individuals, groups, and nations.
All that is necessary is a more thoroughgoing adoption of it. The fallacy at the heart of warfare morality is the supposition that intelligence is to guide men
solely in the attainment of what they happen most to
want; that it has nothing to do with determining
what should be wanted. Intelligence is conceived to
be a kind of corporation lawyer for a captain of desire. It would not be impossible to show that the
natural history of intelligence shows this to be an
erroneous conception. The function of intelligence
has been to find a way out of conflicts by creating a
new end in which the conflicting elements could find
some manner of adjustment. Since a dogmatic
statement must suffice, let it be that the essence of
morality consists in just this application of creative
intelligence to the warfare of ideals.

It is striking that this was thought to be the function of morality by the very man who did more than perhaps any one else to convince the world that struggle for existence is the rule of animal life. "Social Progress," said Huxley in the well-known Romanes Lecture for 1893, "means a checking of the cosmic process at every step and the substitution for it of another, which may be called the ethical process; the end of which is not the survival of those who may happen to be fittest, in respect of the whole conditions which exist, but of those who are ethically the best. . . . The practice of that which is ethically best—what we call goodness or virtue—involves a course of conduct which, in all respects, is opposed to that which leads to success in the cosmic struggle for existence. In place of ruthless self-assertion it demands self-restraint; in place of thrusting aside, or treading down, all competitors, it requires that the individual shall not merely respect, but shall help his fellows; its influence is directed, not so much to the survival of the fittest, as to the fitting of as many as possible to survive."

But as in the case of the recent war, so in the battle over Darwinism, it was those who were in actual touch with the realities of the conflict who kept their heads. So we have from one of the foremost pioneers of evolutionary biology a clean-cut rejection of "evolutionary ethics," while many of the generation of thinkers who experienced only the echoes of the great battle went mad with the idea of applying ultra-Darwinian philosophy to every phase and feature of life. It is from this madness that the coming generations must be saved. The youth of all lands must be led to see a better possibility; must be encouraged to invent the instruments of its actualization; must be assured the opportunity of securing the necessary moral, intellectual, and bodily equipment.

This is not a simple task, but it is a glorious one, and not impossible. "It may seem an audacious proposal," to turn to Huxley once more, "thus to pit the microcosm against the macrocosm and to set man to subdue nature to his higher ends. . . ." And yet, "fragile reed as he may be, man," as Pascal says, "is a thinking reed: there lies within him a fund of energy, operating intelligently and so far akin to that which pervades the universe that it is competent to influence and to modify the cosmic process. In virtue of his intelligence, the dwarf bends the Titan to his will. . . ." Who can review without emotion the long list of man's discoveries and inventions or contemplate unmoved his triumph over all manner of material and social disaster? Neither has man been powerless to change his inheritance from savagery. "The intelligence which has converted the brother of the wolf into the faithful guardian of the flock," not only "ought to be able to do something towards curbing the instincts of savagery in civilized man," but has done so. Savages persist, and may be found even among the best families, but human nature is no longer savage. Except where galling, hopeless conditions of life, too long endured, lead at last to a violent outburst, a course of training, under experts, is required to revive on a large scale the emotional complex characteristic of the ape and tiger stage of human development.

Here, then, is the answer to the contention that might makes right: we will not have it so. We will *make* morality to be something different. Since in morality our chief concern is not a description of things as they are but the realization of things as we would they might be, we will define right and wrong in accordance with the end we seek. And since the end we seek is the completest life for every human being, we will make morality the great instrument for the achievement of that end. Consequently we will say that to act morally is to aim at such an adjustment of conflicting ideals as will secure the greatest proportionate satisfaction of the ideals involved, and to act immorally is to close one's heart to ideals antagonistic to one's own when the two conflict. We will say, Adjustment makes Right. We

will then aim to make such adjustments among the
ideals relevant to the conflicts arising in the nearer
as well as the more remote affairs of life, and will
train youth in this philosophy by having them develop in an environment where the exercise of this
spirit is called for.   And all the while we will more
and more draw upon the inventive genius of men to
create the necessary social apparatus for its wider and
profounder application.

This principle of adjustment is of course far from
novel.   We have applied it again and again and are
now applying it in small things and in great.   There
is no absolute standard in games, yet the rules are
not made in the process of the game by the stronger
forcing his desires upon the weaker player.   Tentative rules are mutually agreed upon, and victory according to these rules determines who wins.   Where
"might" interferes with this arrangement we call it
unclean sport.   There is no absolute legal code, yet
the most powerful of the contestants does not in-
struct the judge and jury and compel a decision in
his favor.   A legal code and a legal procedure, intended to do justice to the merits of the case, have
gradually been evolved and the decision handed down
in conformity with these establishes which contestant
had the superior claim.   Where it is suspected that
might makes right in the law court, we talk of the

perversion of justice and begin to fear for the stability of the commonwealth. The same principle has been applied in the establishment of commissions and arbitration boards of various kinds, in disputes between labor and capital, in conflicts between nations; indeed the history of civilization may be said to be, more than anything else, the record of a struggle to substitute settlement by conciliation for settlement by coercion in one after another sphere of our common life. In testimony of this, social discoveries, quite as wonderful as the great discoveries of science, mark the progress of the centuries from the earliest recorded society to the present. And if there have been periods of retrogression in the direction of savagery—as there have been—this has by no means demonstrated the superiority of coercion over conciliation, but only that good will, estranged for the time being from intelligence, was unable to become incarnate in practical form. It has been the failure to invent the means of adjustment that has led to the use of force. The progeny of reforms resulting from the union of good will and intelligence is enormous, and few people will deny (to adapt James's words) that a vastly greater total number of ideals find shelter in our civilized society than in the older savage ways.

While the discovery of the means of adjusting

conflicting claims has served to enrich life by contributing to the solution of the problem underlying
conflicts, evidence is abundant that the warfare
method has failed in just this respect. The slavery
question, cited to prove the case for might, may serve
us once more. The Civil War did not settle the question of slavery. Settlement of the slavery question
involved the race problem, which was the heart of
the slavery problem. It was dread of the freed negro
that blocked the early emancipation movements in
the South. An indication of this feeling, and at the
same time an attempt to deal with the situation ra-
tionally, was the organization of the African Coloni-
zation Society whose purpose was to remove the freed
negroes to their original African home. The same
sentiment found expression in a letter written by
Madison near the close of his life. He wished he
might have the power of magic. He would exercise
it in turning all negroes white, and thus the slavery
question would be solved in a day. Jefferson, too,
would have been glad to see general emancipation
but for the race aspect of the problem. "As it is,"
he said, "we have the wolf by the ears, and we can
neither hold him, nor safely let him go. Justice is
in one scale, and self-preservation in the other."
Even at the outbreak of the Civil War, the best judgment of the South, as represented by such men as

Lee, recognized slavery as a great evil, but because of the fact of race and color, insisted that sudden emancipation would not solve but complicate the situation. Moreover, by that time slavery had almost burned itself out with progressive soil exhaustion, which would shortly have compelled some form of gradual emancipation.

The Civil War suddenly and violently abolished slavery. But the race problem remained. And the spirit engendered by the war refused to be satisfied with anything short of the social and political equality of black and white. Not even Lincoln, much as he wished to move slowly, could more than moderate the war-hatred of such men as Thaddeus Stevens. The North, flushed with victory, forced upon the South the problem of race equality, with the result that southern feeling toward the negro, which hitherto had been one of benevolent paternalism, was changed to the antipathy of fear. After but ten years of "reconstruction" the North was compelled to recognize that the spirit of might could not solve the negro problem. It retired, leaving the negroes in the hands of a South alienated from them. We enjoy to-day the heritage of this application of warfare morality; the Jim Crow cars, the Grandfather clauses, the lynchings, the race riots, and most serious of all—the militant negro. In short, the race problem, which was the real problem underlying slavery, far from being settled by the war was made more acute than ever. The South still has its wolf by the ears, and a wolf excited to ferocity.

Whatever may be the case with warfare morality as a whole, its emphasis upon self-realization as against the inhibition of desires appears to me sound and most important. Self-respect, not self-denial, is the greatest moral force available. It is not less regard for self we need, but more. The only question is what kind of self is to be respected. Must it necessarily be the self that finds its realization in a mode of life which makes self-realization more difficult if not impossible for others? May it not be the self whose progressive development makes possible the increasing expansion of increasing numbers of other selves? A man in the heat of conflict may rule out of consideration all ideals opposed to his own and those of his group, and act as if in a moral vacuum because, for the time being, the moral order has gone to pieces. But the man who proposes to act morally, or the moral philosopher who is a relativist, has no such liberty. To him *all* ideals are valuable, just because they are some one's ideals. Accordingly, if all of them are not realizable, as in this world they are not, and if no one ideal can be used as a standard, he will aim at an adjustment which sacrifices the

least number. He will say with William James:
The one unconditional commandment is "that we
should seek incessantly, with fear and trembling, so
to vote and act as to bring about the very largest
total universe of good which we can see." And he
will give his active approval to every experiment calculated to discover the means of arriving at this goal
in the concrete issues of life.

It is clear that not every ideal can be realized.
Many must go down. But the fundamental problem
of morality is to secure the richest total of satisfied
desire; and this end is defeated by the encouragement
of a free-for-all fight in which each one looks only
to what he wants. The application of intelligence to
conflicts, with the deliberate purpose of bringing all
relevant ideals into the field of sympathetic appreciation and arriving at an adjustment which gives due
weight to each of the conflicting ideals, even if imperfectly achieved, promises a far better issue than
warfare. "With a little more patience," as Stevenson said, "and a little less temper, a gentler and
wiser method might be found in almost every case;
and the knot that was cut by some fine heady quarrel-
scene . . . might yet have been unwoven by the
hand of sympathy." Working in this spirit man may
yet redeem himself from baseness and misery and
glorify the speck in space we call the earth.

CHAPTER V

RIGHT BY AGREEMENT

No words are more characteristic of human speech than good, bad, right, wrong, and other words of moral appraisal. Obviously these judgments imply an admitted contrast between things as they are and as they ought to be. Yet the course of nature, of which we with all our judgments form a part, is indifferent to these distinctions. The fact has often been pointed out. "Reckless of good and evil," said John Fiske of the method of nature, "it brings forth at once the mother's tender love for her infant and the horrible teeth of the ravening shark, and to its creative indifference the one is as good as the other." Kant put the matter in this form: "If we fix our eyes simply on the course of nature, the ought has no meaning whatever. It is as absurd to ask what nature ought to be as to ask what sort of properties a circle ought to have. The only question we can properly ask is, What comes to pass in nature? just as we can only ask, What actually are the properties of a circle?" Nor need we go to philosophers for this insight. Ask a school-child whether it is not wrong for the sun to rise in the east; whether it ought not rather to rise in the west. The question was put to a nine-year-old boy. He smiled knowingly and ignored the question. When pressed for an answer he scornfully replied: "Say! how do you get that way?"

Nevertheless, from the standpoint of living organisms partisanship is inevitable. Plants appropriate certain substances rather than others; animals prefer certain foods, mates, and breeding places; human beings discover and pursue ideals, thus giving purpose and intelligence to their choices. The selective processes of plants and animals are rudimentary stages in the development of human powers of valuation. They function to preserve life but also to determine what kind of life is to be preserved. Accordingly man, the organism in whom this development has culminated and become aware of itself, does not face the world with indifference. For him the neutral quality of nature breaks up into a hierarchy of things better and worse, as a ray of sunlight, passing through a prism, spreads into a ribbon of colors.

Now since man is constantly made aware of both aspects of his world—of nature as the system of things as they are and of morality as the pattern of

things as they should be—human experience would
seem to be inherently contradictory: Nature, as the
totality of real things, is believed destitute of distinctions based on value, and, at the same time, value
distinctions are believed somehow to be real. In
other words, our minds lodge this interesting inconsistency, that judgments of right and wrong cannot
have, yet certainly do have, reference to genuine features of reality.

Ordinarily logical contraries are companionable
enough bedfellows. There are few minds in which
a goodly number do not sleep quietly side by side.
But they do not fraternize so well in a mind awake.
A mind naturally critical or aroused to reflection
by some crisis is not hospitable to logical inconsistency. One or the other belief is shown the door,
or they are accommodated in separate, incommuni-
cable quarters. So out of the appreciation of the
conflict between the naturalistic and the moral outlook have grown various theories in which the inconsistency we have noticed disappears. We may
suggest some of these. In one of them morality
is declared intrinsically supernatural, and is therefore to be superimposed upon the world of fact.
In another, Nature is the supreme lord of all, and
morality a tissue of sentimentality and fiction. In
a third, "nature" and "morality" are partial aspects

of a whole in which their seeming antagonism is harmonized.

A simple statement of the first position is that of Thomas Dwight, in his *Views of a Catholic Anatomist:* "Perhaps," he says, "we all know atheists who, in despite of logic, lead respectable, pure and useful lives. Let us make much of them; for their children will show themselves more logical. They will join the increasing multitude of those who, knowing no law-giver, see no reason to obey law. What does it matter to them if some other collection of protoplasmic cells suffers a little more or a little less? . . . So having run the gamut of pleasure with other men's money and other men's wives, they will not shrink from the quietus they can so easily make for themselves. They have got bravely over 'the dread of something after death' and are acting accordingly." That is to say, the logic of the natural world is eat, drink, carouse without consideration or restraint, and when the acme of sensuality has been reached, commit suicide. But there is also a supernatural realm, and it has the last word. In that supernatural world men will be punished for allowing themselves to be persuaded by the logic of nature or rewarded for refusing to listen to it. This fact, and this only, makes the good life rational on earth.

While this view escapes the contradiction by making morality superior to nature, the second view escapes by making nature superior to morality. "Man," says Antonio Llano, "exists as a natural and necessary product of universal forces and, like other organic beings, obeys the law of self-expression. . . . It is also a matter of fact that, in pursuing its own interests, every organism constantly finds itself in the presence of other organisms whose interests and welfare cannot but conflict with its own; whence results a struggle wherein the inferior organism must succumb and the superior organism survive and propagate. Whether this condition of affairs be repulsive or shocking, and whether it 'ought' to be different from what it is, are questions no longer to be asked, once we have discarded the old idea of an abitrary will governing the phenomena of nature." The emotional forces of moral idealism, Mr. Llano contends, and the remorse felt when the moral code is violated, are survivals of the pressure and punishments inflicted upon our remote ancestors. "If I consult or scrutinize my conscience," he says, "I find that it is a sort of ghost whose authority is derived from the servility and slavery of my ancestors and whose 'imperative dictates' are the echoes of a state of oppression and superstition against which my present feelings of freedom protest and revolt. I recognize no claims of others on me, no conscience, no obligation. I am my own master." Since each man is an integral part of nature, his wants are likewise integral parts of nature, and are therefore of necessary character. They cannot be reprobated on any moral or rational ground. Hence the only right or justice is natural right or justice, or, in other words, they are names for what serves the interest of the superior organism.

The third way out is found by going behind the scenes. The world of fact and the world of value are declared to be partial expressions of a more comprehensive reality, a reality in the highest sense true and good and beautiful. In this all-harmonizing whole the inconsistent dualism of our everyday standpoint is gathered up and unified. Thus Plato taught that the things which seem solid and final to our common-sense analysis are but imperfect, fleeting presentations on the temporal and spatial stage of mortal life, of perfect, eternal types whose locus is a transcendental realm, and that the very purpose of the finite appearance of the eternal objects is to serve the supreme reality of all, the Good. The position is well stated by Emerson: "The Times, as we say, the present aspect of our social state, the Laws, Divinity, Natural Science, Agriculture, Art, Trade, Letters, have their root in an invisible spiritual reality. To appear in these aspects they must first exist or have some necessary foundation. Besides all the small reasons we assign [we professors of this or that, we politicians, we editors, we social reformers], there is a great reason for every extant fact; a reason which lies grand and immovable, often unsuspected behind it in silence." To this great silent reason we must go for the adequate explanation of the world that is, for moral idealism, for the struggle between them.

And what do we find? We find each to perform a necessary function; for ultimate reality, the Oversoul, "in which we rest as the earth lies in the soft arms of the atmosphere," is moral. Now in the Over-soul as Over-soul there can be no obstacles, no ideals, no conflicts. But without these morality is impossible. If, then, ultimate reality is moral this morality can only be achieved through the enactment of a moral drama on a finite stage. Hence the stage we call nature, the actors we call men, the drama we call life. From the finite view the conflict between the *is* and the *ought* is real and necessary, and the inconsistency is fact. But, says Emerson, "the dice of God are always loaded." Seen under the aspect of eternity, the inconsistency disappears. All is harmony, peace, and the eternal triumph of right.

We may say, I think, that accredited moral theories fall into one of these three patterns. Therefore, widely as they may differ in other respects, they agree in one important principle: they agree that the moral life demands conformity with a preexisting standard; i.e., each implies the existence of an order of things which is the repository of all real worth, and that conduct takes its rating from positive or negative relation to this supreme worthiness. This is obviously true of the first pattern; true, if not obviously true, of the third; and it is implied in the second, since conventional morality is there reduced to an illusion on the ground that nature should be the sole criterion of conduct. This common agreement suggests the possibility of a fourth type which, however it may differ or not differ in other respects, parts company with all other types at just this point. A theory which, instead of making the moral life dependent upon a previously existing moral order, makes the moral order dependent upon a previously existing moral life. The remainder of this chapter shall be devoted to outlining this position.

Perhaps the most elemental fact connected with the moral life is the existence of impulse. Without beings who are instinctively active, who naturally think things and do things for the sake of

thinking and doing them, or, better, because they
are made that way, it is difficult to see how anything like right or wrong could ever come to be.
Even granting the eternal existence of a perfect
moral code in the mind of an absolute being or in
some transcendental region, this would only mean
the theoretical or possible existence of morality.
Right and wrong in their true inwardness and actuality would not exist until some thought or deed
occurred to be in harmony with or in violation of
the eternal standard. We may consequently conclude that the raw material of moral conduct is
the impulsive life of man.

Morality is dependent not only upon impulse, but
upon conflict between impulses. What could be
meant by calling an impulse right or wrong if its
satisfaction had no bearing whatever upon any other
want or need? If impulses were insulated from
one another so that the satisfaction of one had no
bearing on the rest, if impulses were not "members
of one body," mutual sharers in a common destiny
determinable to some extent by each, what would
a moral problem be? For even a transcendental
creed is vital only if it succeeds in making contact
with some natural human impulse which will be
satisfied if the creed is observed and thwarted if

it is not observed. Impulses running counter to each other are therefore presupposed in morality.

All human beings, however, are creatures with impulses running counter to each other. There is the impulse to accumulate and the impulse to spend; the impulse to wander and the impulse to stay at home; the impulse to enjoy a family and the impulse to retain the freedom of the unmarried; the impulse to make the moments count and the impulse to dawdle away the time; the impulse to believe only what is true and the impulse to believe true only what is pleasant. Who can name the sum of antitheses of this sort? William James has put the situation well. "The actually possible in this world," he said, "is vastly narrower than the demanded; and there is always a *pinch* between the ideal and the actual which can only be got through by leaving part of the ideal behind. There is hardly a good which we can imagine except as competing for the possession of the same bit of space and time with some other imagined good. Every end of desire that presents itself appears exclusive of some other end or desire. Shall a man drink and smoke, *or* keep his nerves in condition?—he cannot do both. Shall he follow his fancy for Amelia, *or* Henrietta?—both cannot be the choice of his heart. Shall he have the dear old Republican party, *or* a spirit of unsophistication in public affairs?—he cannot have both, etc."

And the whole story is not told in one's own desires. There are the equally multitudinous desires of others. As desires are not insulated from one another so people are not insulated from one another. Theoretically, morality is conceivable if given one individual whose desires conflict, but it would be a pale affair compared with the practical actuality. It is the fact that other people also make demands upon life and that these have a direct bearing on the demands we make, which is responsible for the real rub in the situation.

Human life may thus be said to present a "howling mob of desires, each struggling to get breathing-room for the ideal to which it clings." The result is that choice is made inevitable; and this, the necessity of choosing, lays the foundation of the moral life.

Lays the foundation only, for without the presence of another factor morality would still be out of the question. That factor we may call intelligence, using a word which is unfortunately most vague and ambiguous in current speech. Let it for the moment involve at least this much: (a) That human beings can act with an awareness of their action; (b) that they can act deliberately or purposively, that is, act because they want specifically what the action will secure; (c) that they are not limited to action which is its own immediate incentive but can act from a desire for remoter ends the attainment of which is dependent upon the present action as means. Intelligence means, negatively, liberation from routine response to environment, and, positively, the power to deal with environment imaginatively. So much, at least. It must be clear that without this capacity the exercise of choice, in any proper sense of the word, cannot take place. Competition between diverse tendencies to act are observable in the animal world, and the conflict is often resolved in favor of one of the contending impulses, but the issue is decided by the passive, not the active, selection of one alternative in preference to others. That is one reason why man can evolve a moral life and animals cannot.

This brings us to what we may designate the culminating function of intelligence in morality— the positing of a more or less comprehensive end for the sake of which other ends are to be attained or sacrificed, and the discovery of ways and means for bringing about the desired consummation. Where it is not possible to control instinctive and habitual promptings with design there can be no

moral life. That is our final reason for never calling animals moral or immoral, even when we believe them to show the rudiments out of which
morality may have developed. "A struggle may
often be observed in animals between different instincts," as Darwin remarks, "or between an instinct
and some more habitual disposition; as when a dog
rushes after a hare, is rebuked, pauses, hesitates,
pursues again, or returns ashamed to his master;
or as between the love of a female dog for her
young puppies and for her master—for she may
be seen to slink away to them, as if half ashamed
of not accompanying her master." But there the
matter ends. A dog never sits down to reflect on
his conduct nor tries to figure out what a sensible
dog, in view of the competing dog-satisfactions, had
better strive for. And he never arrives at an ideal
of dog-life to serve as a guide for the adjustment
of a particular conflict of desires.

Similarly, a very young child, reaching out for
a forbidden object, may slap his disobedient hand
with the other, and emphatically say, "No, no; no,
no." Doubtless out of just such conflicts the moral
consciousness develops; but we have no ground for
believing that when young children decide issues
of this sort they have before them an ideal of conduct. Therefore, while children are constantly con-

fronted with what to the adult are moral situations, they are not held to be "morally responsible." We wait until they have reached "years of discretion"; until we believe them able actively to espouse a program of life. For only then do they possess the power to act on the moral plane.

Given a being, then, who is spontaneously active, whose impulses and desires conflict among themselves and with those of others, who can become aware of his actions, his wants, and the conflicting interests in which he is involved, who can manipulate the situation with reference to a projected goal, and you have a potentially moral being. What, now, turns this potency into fact? What is the connotation of the word moral?

Well, first of all, the moral man is one who, facing the complexity of competing impulses and desires, proposes to arrive at some sort of adjudication. A degree and kind of adjudication is, of course, inevitable. In the total absence of it human life is inconceivable. Each of us grows up in a family and subject to various group pressures; each of us lives in a community, and must have dealings with others. Each of us is thus compelled to adopt some give and take basis for conduct. But I mean something over and above, something deeper than this. I mean the positive devotion to a manner of life. A recent announcement speaks in this wise of a celebrated author: "He is not a radical, nor a Puritan, nor a moralist, but an artist of high degree, and the true artist is not concerned with morality, religion nor patriotism." The sentence is rather ambiguous, but it may be taken to mean that the artist is not concerned with the conflict in which the common man is involved; that he is above it, or stands aside from it. If so taken, it describes the very antithesis of the moral attitude.

To be moral is to have a program of life. Therefore those who are indifferent to the conflict of human demands and purposes, even if they happen to observe the catalogue of virtues, do not illustrate the spirit called moral. Neither is this spirit illustrated by those who make the succession of impulses the order of life, or who act on the doctrine, in any of its various forms, that right is a name for whatever can be gotten away with. Morality is neither a capitulation nor a spree. If it does not involve facing the promptings of life with the purpose of fashioning them to an ideal it involves nothing whatsoever, and is a word without meaning. Morality is an art; it demands creativeness, and it demands dedication and discipline.

But the definition remains as yet too general. Devotion to a goal of life is not the full definition

of the moral attitude, nor is discipline aimed at for
its own sake. The moral life demands devotion
to a specific kind of goal and discipline in the interest of that goal. What goal, then?

For the answer we must return to consider once
more the proposition that the raw material of moral
conduct is the impulsive life of man. According
to some people, as B. L. Taylor once said, "one
would think that in the beginning God created a set
of principles, and man was without form and void."
We have rejected this view. We have taken the
position that chronologically wants come first and
the moral life afterwards. It is hardly possible to
make this point too plain. What men want is,
just because they want it, good. Wants are their
own justification; they cannot be justified by anything else. If wants did not clash, so that all wants
could be satisfied without interference, life would
be found all good. Not that all desires would then
be right, or that it would always be right to desire
what we desired. Desires, as desires, are neither
right nor wrong; they simply are. In a world where
all desires could be satisfied immediately and without involving later dissatisfaction, the concepts right
and wrong, and the words good and bad, in the
moral sense, would have no significance.

Very well. This forces us a step further. Man's

impulses and desires are prior not only chronologically but logically, and, if I may say so, morally. Let us be quite specific also about this. Morality is a means for the satisfaction of human wants. In other words, morality must justify itself at the bar of life, not life at the bar of morality. While emphasizing this point, let us not neglect the parallel fact to be taken immediately with it—that human impulses present a complex intrication of competing wants which, in the very nature of the case, cannot all be satisfied. With these two facts before us, namely, the primacy of desires and the impossibility of satisfying all of them, we are in a position to state the goal of the moral life. It is the richest possible attainment of satisfied wants. To which had better be added at once that by this is meant not a settled, fixed quantum, but a progressive approximation, changing and growing with times and conditions, to the fullest realization of personal potentialities and the completest possible participation in the appealing interests of life. Dedication to this end is the essence of moral purpose, and the fashioning of one's life in accord with this purpose is moral discipline.

Taken in abstraction from the preceding discussion this statement of the moral goal may be interpreted in an individual or in a collective sense.

It should naturally be taken with its context, and therefore in a collective sense. If wants are their own justification, the accidental fact that they are the wants of diverse people can make no theoretical difference. But the wants of others must be included in the moral aim along with one's own wants not only for theoretical reasons, but because they actually form part of every one's wants. Since this is what the position comes to, it must face the popular objection that all acts, when examined, turn out to be selfish acts. According to this view, no one ever acts or can act from any motive but self-satisfaction. Even where a person lays down his life for another he does it because it gives him satisfaction so to do. He acts out of regard for himself. There is doubtless a glint of truth in this contention. All acts, in so far as they are voluntary, are self-expressive or have their source in the self. Even when done under compulsion they are yet his acts if they represent his choice under the circumstances. But though every act is self-expressive, it is not necessarily self-centered. Acts have a source and a termination. The source is always the acting self, but the termination may be either the acting self or another self. A father may bring home something to eat which suits his own taste but is liked by no other member of the family, or he may bring home something he does not himself care for but of which the other members of the family are especially fond. Whatever the ultimate psychological explanation may be, these two acts cannot be reduced to the same category.

The reply may be made that in the latter case he does it after all because he likes to, and so to please himself. He does it because he likes to, but not necessarily to please himself. In rare instances the latter may be true; more often, however, the act is less sophisticated, being a direct response to the thought of the family. It is anticipation of the pleased family, not anticipation of the pleased self which impels to the action. We easily overlook this fact because of our superficial analysis, and because of our inveterate tendency to explain spontaneous activity by sophisticated causes—or is phrases the better word? Whether this explanation is conclusive or not, the thought of the condition of other people is in any case the spring of action. Were human beings emotionally indifferent to each other, morality would necessarily be a purely personal affair. Since men can and actually do include the wants of others in their range of interests, the good life must be defined in collective terms. Unnumbered desires, one's own desires and those of others, each with a valid claim to satisfaction, and many of them running counter to one another so that some manner of adjustment is inevitable—this it is which sets the stage for the moral life. And the moral person is one who in the presence of this situation is actuated by a desire which the immoral person is without, a desire to make some contribution to the richest attainment of desire for every one.

It has been suggested that the problem may be simplified by reducing the number of desires to be counted worthy of consideration. The Epicureans assigned to the satisfaction of some desires (the pleasures of the intellect, of the feelings, of the moral sentiments) a much higher value as pleasures than to those of others (pleasures of the senses). John Stuart Mill later defended this view with clearness and force. "Of two pleasures," he said, "if there be one to which all or almost all who have experience of both give a decided preference, irrespective of any feeling of moral obligation to prefer it, that is the more desirable pleasure." And he felt it to be an unquestionable fact that this test proved the employment of the higher faculties on the whole the most conducive to happiness. "Few human creatures," he contended, "would consent to be changed into any of the lower animals, for a promise of the fullest allowance of a beast's pleas-

ures; no intelligent human being would consent to
be a fool, no instructed person would be an igno-
ramus, no person of feeling and conscience would be
selfish and base, even though they should be persuaded that the fool, the dunce, or the rascal is
better satisfied with his lot than they are with theirs.
They would not resign what they possess more than
he for the most complete satisfaction of all the
desires which they have in common with him."
Owing to this peculiar pleasure of the higher satisfactions, "it is better to be a human being dissatisfied
than a pig satisfied; better to be Socrates dissatisfied
than a fool satisfied. And if the fool, or the pig,
is of a different opinion, it is because they only
know their own side of the question."

The argument, however, is open to the objection
that the other party to the comparison does not
know both sides either. "For example," says Paul
Janet, "a common debauchee or a greedy speculator
might despise the pleasures of science, art, virtue;
but they are incompetent judges, Mr. Mill tells
us; they have never experienced the pleasures which
they despise. Very good—but may not the argument be applied conversely? Would a St. Vincent
de Paul or a Newton be competent to estimate, if
they despised sensual pleasures, the delights of wild
passions? Might not libertines maintain that a life

of pleasure has joys of infinite profundity which ascetics or pedants are incapable of appreciating?" E. B. McGilvary makes the same objection: "It is better to be a Socrates unsatisfied—better for whom! For Socrates or for the pig? But a pig! Who would be a pig? Is he not loathly? Assuredly he is—*to us;* but to *himself* not so assuredly. Who knows what preciousness there may be to pigs in unadulterated piggery?" And one who believes that the sole purpose of morality is to serve as a means for securing what men actually want cannot but endorse these criticisms. There is no one superior desire and no one set of desires which may be adopted as standard.

Holding to this conclusion, some way must be found for the adjustment of desires. And there are three alternative methods practically available for deciding which desires shall have the right of way: we may let the desires fight it out; we may appeal to some authority external to the desires; or we may come to some agreement as between desires. In view of our discussion, the third method is the only acceptable one. In harmony with this alternative we will then define the moral spirit (meaning to be understood in the best sense) as a genuine willingness to play the game of life according to the rules which will make it the most rich in satisfaction; and we will define right as a rule of that game.

It is altogether too plain that many people will reject any such concept outright. The suggestion of a similarity between the moral life and a *game*, no matter *what* sort of game, will be so obnoxious to them that they will refuse to enter into the matter any further. Yet at this point no compromise is permissible. We must take our stand that the moral spirit has closer kinship with art than with business. If the people wedded to the reverse idea will see in this the reduction of life to a frolic and morality to verbiage, that is a consequence we must accept. We can only declare our innocence of any such intention. We have specifically rejected the notion that people can live together happily by regarding life either as an idle pastime or as an orgy or frivolity free from any obligation other than to seek the fullest liberation of undisciplined impulse. There are certain conclusions, however, which the view we have arrived at carries with it. These cannot be surrendered without giving up the view itself. First of all, as already intimated, morality is a means, not the end. The end is life replete with the joy of living. Moral rules can therefore only be those regulations which justify themselves experimentally to be serviceable in securing that end. It follows that the whole set of moral concepts must be regarded as approximate and tentative, to be superseded by ones better able to further the ends of life as conditions change and man's inventive imagination develops.

But what rules, concretely, can secure this end? In the nature of the case the answer to this question cannot be conclusive. Yet neither are we left utterly in the dark. We are not compelled to start *ab initio*. We begin with life in progress. There is a fund of human experience to draw upon. Certain acts have been discovered to defeat life, others to advance it. All this we find operative as custom or institution or ideal. Starting with the morality in vogue, we get a sense of the venture in which man, as a moral being, is engaged, and this is the beginning of moral wisdom. If the approved conventions thus espoused are recognized for what they are—funded human experience, in which are preserved, along with the insight, the restricted outlook of the past—we shall be in no danger of accepting them passively. On the contrary, we shall feel under obligation to find for them an ever broader, deeper, more unique significance. John Dewey is right: "Loyalty to whatever in the established environment makes a life of excellence possible is the beginning of all progress. The best we can accomplish for posterity is to transmit unimpaired and with some increment of meaning the environment that makes it possible to maintain the habits of decent and refined life."

In the second place, while wants are individually unique, it is possible to classify them in groups, somewhat as animals and plants, always exhibiting individual differences, may be classified as genera and species. No such arrangement can be perfect or suitable for all persons and times, but it can serve as a practical simplification of the problem of adjustment. Suppose, for example, we reduce the various desires of men to five general types: for food and shelter, comradeship, occupation or work, sex relation, and change. It may be objected, and very properly, that food, shelter, comradeship, sex, change, have widely different meanings as they are actually wanted by different people, and that, moreover, the relative emphasis on one or the other must vary from case to case and from time to time. From the standpoint of our general contention this is not a slight, but a very important consideration, but it does no damage to the position. Morality, as we have said, is an art, and no more demands of all men devotion to the same identical wants and an equal devotion to each, than art demands of the painter the use of the same identical colors and an equal quantity of each. It demands the very opposite. The bringing together of the various desires into a coöperative venture is in each case to be an original accomplishment, but this does not mean the elimination of all relation to like ventures of others. The essential thing is that we aim at, and, as far as conditions permit, achieve, a manner of life which makes possible, with ever richer meaning, the satisfaction of the common desire for food and shelter, for human fellowship, for self-expression in work regarded as worth doing, for sex relationship, for diversion or change. This is a feasible plan and it moves in the direction of the moral ideal.

Finally, the ideal here suggested is not intended in a universal or abstract sense. It is not something esoteric. It has reference to the activities in which men and women are engaged from day to day and to the relations which they bear to those whom their lives can be discovered to touch. So to act that in each case the richest satisfaction of every one is realized is a sheer impossibility. We do not know what this would be and we have no way of finding out. But we can see some distance into the ramifications of our acts, and it is sufficient that we count in the wants we can actually discover to be affected, provided we are really trying to see as far as we can. One of the early students of human behavior complained that men were quick to declare their love of God whom they had never seen, while they showed no love of their fellows whom they saw every day. It was an old story even in John's day for people to be fanatically devoted to abstract or remote virtues and to betray them daily in their concrete and immediate form.

Neither does moral excellence require a perfect balance of the wants thus discoverable. This too is impossible, except in terms of a formula which surrenders its life to be canonized. But we can, if we will, discover approximately what the more appealing desires at issue are, and we can do considerable to promote their realization. It is by no means impossible—if we have a mind to do it—to make life richer in satisfactory content within the radius of our activities and influence. Devotion to this ideal, deliberately espoused because of its superior power to develop personality and add to the joy of living, is the essence of moral purpose in this theory which refuses to seek its pattern in nature or in the supernatural.

CHAPTER VI

THE SELF

WHAT is there a man is more certain of than that he is himself and not some one else? One does not anticipate any great difficulty in describing what this self is—until one makes the attempt. But when the attempt is made it turns out to be a formidable undertaking. So that as a matter of fact the people who are most certain that they know what the self is are the people who have never stopped to think about it. Those who have thoroughly studied the subject admit great difficulty in determining how much or how little is to be included in the concept. It is possible to say with reasonable completeness what a chair is, or a house, or a cloud; but that most intimate thing of all appears to baffle description. Samuel Butler states the case in this way:

"We regard our personality as a simple definite whole; as a plain, palpable, individual thing, which can be seen going about the streets or sitting indoors at home, which lasts us our lifetime, and about the confines of which no doubt can exist in the minds ot reasonable people. But in truth this 'we,' which looks so simple and definite, is a nebulous and indefinable aggregation of component parts which war not a little among themselves, our perception of our existence at all being perhaps due to this very clash of warfare, as our sense of sound and light is due to the jarring of vibrations." And these component parts of the self, he goes on to suggest, "blend some of them so imperceptibly into, and are so inextricably linked on to, outside things which clearly form no part of our personality, that when we try to bring ourselves to book, and determine wherein we consist, or to draw a line as to where we begin or end, we find ourselves completely baffled. There is nothing but fusion and confusion."

This introduces us to the first difficulty encountered in an attempt to define the self. It is hard to say where to begin or end. To many people it seems obvious that every individual is in some sense his parents, grandparents, great-grandparents, and so on, or, as Lafcadio Hearn expresses it, "countless millions of dead in one life manifestation." But if he is these, is he not also his children, grandchildren, great-grandchildren, and so on? We cannot accept as decisive the psychological fact that common-sense people are more accustomed to think of the self as trailing back through their ancestors but not as projecting forward through their descendants. They think in just the reverse way in the matter of immortality, believing it to have only future extension, and not (unless they happen to be theosophists or something of the sort) continuity into the past.

The self must thus be regarded as a kind of storehouse or depot, where life collects experience and redistributes it to life. Once started on this tack, however, there seems no logical stopping place in the ramifications of the self. That is why Butler feels inclined to identify the self with the race, or even with the entire tree of life, and Edward Carpenter cannot stop short of the conclusion that there is but one Self throughout the universe. "It is hidden in all living things, men and animals and plants; it pervades all creation. In everything that has consciousness it is the self; it watches over all operations, it overshadows all creatures, it moves in the depths of our hearts, the perceiver, the only being that is cognizant of all and yet free from all."

There is another and very different obstacle to the discovery of the self. The self refuses to be discovered. David Hume made a diligent search, and he could only find a bundle or collection of perceptions, but no self. His statement is famous:

"For my part, when I enter most intimately into what I call *myself*, I always stumble on some particular perception or other, of heat or cold, light or shade, love or hatred, pain or pleasure. I never catch *myself* at any time without a perception, and never can observe anything but the perception. When my perceptions are removed for any time, as by sound sleep, so long am I insensible of *myself*, and may truly be said not to exist. And were all my perceptions removed by death, and could I neither think, nor feel, nor see, nor love, nor hate after the dissolution of my body, I should be entirely annihilated, nor do I conceive what is farther requisite to make me a perfect nonentity. If any one, upon serious and unprejudiced reflection, thinks he has a different notion of *himself*, I must confess I can no longer reason with him."

Other thinkers, utterly out of sympathy with Hume's method, have likewise found the self quite elusive. They have pointed out that in all our searching and finding what we seek slips from us and looks on as it were over our shoulder. If we turn suddenly to catch this observer, we find that the object of our search has had notice of our purpose, has eluded our grasp, and vanished behind our new position. So we may play hide and seek down an infinite regress of dodgings only to be forced to confess at last that the unobserved observer is observing our defeat.

The fact seems to be that whether we seek to

discover the bounds of the self by tracing its extension outwards, or, turning our attention inwards,
attempt to plumb its nature by sounding the depths
of our being, we are frustrated in the attempt.

Possibly we may fare better if instead of asking
directly what the self is we ask how it comes to be.
Most people would admit that there was a time
when it did not exist. And doubtless the way in
which certain organic individuals, as distinguished
from others, naturally respond to their environment
and thus form what we may call their predisposition
or individuality, offers a hint. Even animals show
individuality in this sense. Lovers of dogs in particular are fond of calling attention to this, but all
students of animal life are soon struck by the fact
that, while as a matter of human convenience, we
may speak of the uniformity of animal behavior,
strictly speaking they exhibit all manner of interesting, unique deviations. An example suggesting the
truth is recorded by a sympathetic witness:

"As I stood on the bank of the brook, a fine little
song-sparrow hopped about within two yards of me,
getting his feet wet nipping seeds from the dry
foliage along the water's edge. Another song-sparrow chirped excitedly from the other bank as if
warning the first of my presence. And the one on
my side chirped calmly back as if to say: 'Don't

be silly; I see him all right. He's harmless. Come on over.' And presently he did come over and also searched for seeds, but at a safe distance and keeping up a constant, nervous chirp of danger. Finally, losing courage altogether, he flew farther down the stream. The other meanwhile hopped to a limb within a few feet of my face and eyed me calmly, first with one eye and then with the other, uttering a low little peep which said, 'See! I'm not afraid,' until suddenly he broke into the rippling song which in our country is the first dependable signal that spring is once more abroad in our valley."

In children these differences in natural disposition and temperament are marked, and they would be still more noticeable and various if the routine behavior demanded by adults did not suppress and conceal them.

No doubt organic individuality has much to do with the self, but it is not the self. How then does the self arise out of the interaction of native capacity and environmental conditions? The question is not easy to answer because in few instances does the self have a birthday. It is true that here and there a person recalls the first moment of self-awareness as one of the dramatic experiences of life, as the university student who gives this vivid account: "I remember very clearly when the first realization came to me. I do not remember the circumstances; it was, I believe, a conversation between my father and mother, which aroused deep feeling in me, made me very happy or miserable, I forget which. I stretched up my arms and wanted to shout at the sheer joy of being alive. Perhaps I did. It came all at once, like a revelation: *I am myself!*" But this is unusual. As a rule, people looking back to a time when they first puzzled about the self, find it already a constituent part of the recollection. The instance recorded by an American philosopher is a far more common type:

"What I believe to be my earliest memory is of a sultry summer day in a room where a brother and a sister were at play while I sat withdrawn on a bench at the window. A white china dish with a bar of yellow soap was on the window sill, and the panes were covered with moisture so that the sun shone through yellowed and sicklied. I remember gazing curiously at the soiled gingham dress I wore, at the stocking crumpled down over the shoe. A strange irrational loneliness had laid hold on me, and the ugliness of the soap, the distressful yellow sun, the incomprehensible self in the incomprehensible gingham dress, all gradually merged into a vague and desolate wonder, how could I be I, so helplessly small in the midst of a big unmindful world."

But even where the first awareness of self may
be dated, the circumstances of its genesis are generally recalled in so vague and sketchy a manner
that little can be deduced as to the conditions under
which the self is first made manifest. Fortunately,
a few people remember these circumstances with
sufficient clearness to make it possible for us to get
some clew as to the origin and possibly also the nature of the self. And one of the very best records
is found in Edmund Gosse's *Father and Son:*

"In our little back-garden, my Father had built
up a rockery for ferns and mosses, and from the
water supply of the house he had drawn a leaden
pipe so that it pierced upwards through the rockery
and produced, when a tap was turned, a pretty sil-
very parasol of water. The pipe was exposed somewhere near the foot of the rockery. One day two
workmen, who were doing some repairs, left their
tools during the dinner-hour in the back-garden, and
as I was marching about I suddenly thought that to
see whether one of these would make a hole in
the pipe would be attractive. It did make such a
hole, quite easily, and then the matter escaped my
mind. But a day or two afterwards, when my father
came in to dinner, he was very angry. He had
turned the tap, and, instead of the fountain arching
at the summit, there had been a rush of water

through a hole at the foot. The rockery was absolutely ruined.

"Of course I realized in a moment what I had done, and I sat frozen with alarm, waiting to be denounced. But my mother remarked on the visit of the plumbers two or three days before, and my Father instantly took up the suggestion. No doubt that was it; the mischievous fellows had thought it amusing to stab the pipe and spoil the fountain. No suspicion fell on me; no question was asked of me. I sat there, turned to stone within, but outwardly sympathetic and with unchecked appetite. . . .

"But of all the thoughts which rushed upon my savage and undeveloped little brain at this crisis, the most curious was that I had found a companion and confidant in myself. There was a secret in this world and it belonged to me and to somebody who lived in the same body with me. There were two of us and we could talk with one another. It is difficult to define impressions so rudimentary, but it is certain that it was in this dual form that the sense of my individuality now suddenly descended upon me, and it is equally certain that it was a great solace to me to find a sympathizer in my own breast."

This record furnishes a clew. The self takes its rise from the development of independent interests.

These interests may be things, schemes, secrets, or what not. It is the activity of appropriation, of adoption as one's own, and the consequent feeling of proprietorship, which mark the genesis of the self. One of the first, if not indeed the first, clean-cut feelings to take shape in the early life of the child is the feeling mine. John Dewey's "I own, therefore I am" is better psychology than Descartes' "I think, therefore I am." At first the child lays claim to anything and everything with a divine disregard of conditions. Soon, however, his claims come into opposition with the like claims of others, and out of such conflicts eventually issues self-awareness. That is why when this awareness occurs it appears to supervene; to catch up with the self. "We awake and find ourselves on a stair," said Emerson; "there are stairs below us, which we seem to have ascended; there are stairs above us, many a one, which go upward and out of sight." The dawn of self-consciousness gradually reveals a complexity of things, people, memories, powers, capacities, likes, dislikes, plans, hopes, all saturated with a kind of centrality of reference; all related to each other by the feeling of belonging together.

We are accustomed to think of the self as the unfoldment of an inborn portion of human nature, or as a core of psychic being upon which impres-

sions are impinged from without much as an apple
may be stuck full of cloves. In truth, it is something very different. It is a center of energy, a
going-concern, acting and being acted upon, which
gradually came into existence as the native impulsive life of the individual was organized into mean-
ingful habits under stress of a social and physical
environment. It is a fluctuating collection of desires, memories, aptitudes, hopes, and the like,
which, as a result of the give-and-take relationship
of an active organism and an active environment,
have come to keep house together in the same body
and are there felt to be members of one family.

Looked at in this way the self loses much of its
traditional mysteriousness. It is no longer a mystery why the exact extensiveness of the self is so
difficult to determine. As a matter of everyday observation human beings instinctively become attached to all manner of things, and so warmly and
intimately that the fortune of these is regarded as
the fate of the self. In the widest sense, a man's
self includes, as William James has indicated, all
those things which "if they wax and prosper, he
feels triumphant; if they dwindle and die away,
he feels cast down—not necessarily in the same degree for each thing, but in much the same way for
all." And who can say how much this may include?

Our body must be counted in; for what is more inseparable from the concept of a person than, say, his gait, his smile, his physical mannerisms, or even his bulk? Is Hamlet's self thinkable in the Falstaff's body, or Falstaff's in Hamlet's? "Our father and mother," we would agree, "our wife and babes, are bone of our bone and flesh of our flesh. When they die a part of our very selves is gone. If they do anything wrong, it is our shame. If they are insulted, our anger flashes forth as readily as if we stood in their place." Our country, our home, our belongings, are owned with different degrees of intimacy. And there are few people who, "if a life-long construction of their hands or brains were suddenly swept away, would not feel a shrinkage of personality, a partial reduction of themselves to nothingness." There is literally nothing which may not be regarded as belonging to the self by some one.

It is to Hume's credit that at a time when it was not easy to do so he clearly appreciated the inseparability of the self from its processes, from its active powers and capacities, its likes and dislikes, its fears and aspirations. His recognition of this fact gives to his statement even to-day the ring of reality. But in his anxiety to emphasize diversity of content he slighted the equally real unity of the diverse elements. He admitted that they were associated; spoke of them as a bundle or collection; and referred to certain laws of association to account for their being linked as they are. This, however, is not enough. They are not only associated, but felt to be associated. And the togetherness of feelings is by no means the same thing as the feeling of their togetherness. Consequently, many readers who have found his treatment fresh and suggestive, have turned away from it because the very essence of the self seemed to be left out.

But, again, no mystery need be made of the matter. Hume simply failed to give due weight to an important aspect of the self. The kinship of the constituent elements is as much a fact as the elements themselves. Only it is not an occult fact, an interjection from another region. Unique as the color of the fringed gentian or the taste of grape fruit, it is nevertheless a fragment of concrete experience, as they are. The answer to the question, how this can be, depends upon how far we insist on going. Ultimately, we must confess ignorance, yet there is an answer in our range. The constituents of the self interpenetrate and are felt to belong together because they are all functions of the same organism.

The most puzzling characteristic of the self, its elusiveness, may be dealt with in the same manner.

The material of the self is not fixed but fluctuating. It therefore gets arranged into different patterns, and no single pattern exhausts the whole self. A very slight thing, as we all know, may substitute one self for another, as in the following instance, which could be duplicated by any of us:

"To-day, in the woods, I passed a deserted saw-mill. I found it with my nose, for it is still haunted by the odor of pine. And between the time I lifted my right foot and put it down, I had traveled along that smell four thousand miles and was young again. You and I were back tramping in the Black Forest, laying great plans to win the world to better ways. The old feeling of life's meaningfulness, the old sense of dedication, possessed me. My whole being was a-tingle with energy and idealism. But a tin lizzie rattled around a bend in the road and I was instantly reduced to the battered remnant of a man I have become since those golden days."

The point needs no elaboration. What is better known than that we are different selves to different people and in different relationships? And who that is honest has not often felt with Paul—"For the good that I would I do not; but the evil which I would not, that I do"? Now while these various selves may live their separate lives before men, they all foregather in memory, and, consequently, if any of them attempts to set up an exclusive claim, the rest object. This does something to explain why, no matter what we select as representative of the self, we cannot shake off the feeling that the self is somehow outside the circle we have drawn.

A second reflection takes us a distance further, and accounts for the most tantalizing feeling of all, the feeling that no matter by what clever ruse we attempt to trap the self we never succeed in meeting face to face, though it seems to be all the while at our very elbow. The explanation is simple, and convincing, after a little thought. The search for the self may itself become the object of interest. When that is the case, the various selves successively become objects of awareness, as anything else may. Each of them is accordingly tinged with the feeling of being owned or appropriated. Through our in'veterate habit of thinking in images or of carrying images along with our thinking, an image is created to symbolize this activity of appropriation, and we thus get an onlooker at our back whom we can never surprise out of that position.

There is one phase of the problem which we have not as yet examined. Granted that the self is here correctly described, how shall we explain the practically universal conviction that there is a *true* self distinct from the more or less superficial self which from time to time and from situation to situation may appear as the true self's representative or substitute or screen? Any one who has criticized himself, has been ashamed of himself, struggled to rid himself of a desire, a memory, or a habit—and who has not?—has experienced the division. And aside from such fleeting experiences, all men are more or less aware of an innermost, a deeper, a truer self which does the driving, although shallower selves may get their hands on the reins. So W. H. Hudson was a deeper self when abroad in a wind, especially galloping on horseback. The wind, he said, transforms me "into a new and different being, one as unlike my ordinary self as, say, a sparrow-hawk is unlike a barn-door fowl." And William James describes his more central self in a letter: "I have often thought that the best way to define a man's character would be to seek out the particular mental or moral attitude in which, when it came upon him, he felt himself most deeply and intensely active and alive. At such moments there is a voice inside which speaks and says: 'This is the real me!' " And he adds: "Now as well as I can describe it, this characteristic attitude in me always involves an element of active tension, a holding of my own, as it were, and trusting outward things to perform their part so as to make it a full

harmony, but without any *guaranty* that they will.
Make it a guaranty—and the attitude immediately
becomes to my consciousness stagnant and stingless."

But once more we are in a position to remove
the veil of mystery. Some interest or set of interests, some experiences or memories or hopes are
felt more intensely than others; they are dearer,
more intimate, warmer; in them the quality of being owned is more pungent and keen. There is no
impropriety in calling this the truer self. It *is* the
truer self. Of all that which is flavored with the
self-feeling *it* has the flavor in fullest saturation.
As certain people may call forth more warmth of
affection, as one friend may be the dearest friend,
so may one self. The validity of this analysis is
supported by those individuals for whom there remain two or more sets of interests, memories, and
plans, which will not be unified. They are recognized as dual or multiple persons, whether they are
ordinary mortals like Stevenson's familiar creation
or renowned thinkers like George Santayana, in
whom, as Margaret Münsterberg has aptly said,
"the naturalistic philosopher and the devout poet
stand gazing at each other across an abyss that cannot be bridged."

Perhaps something needs to be said lest the re-
moval of mystery to which reference has repeatedly

been made be misunderstood.   Mystery remains, and will always remain.   How human selves can arrive in the realm called nature and, having arrived, survive, if only for a season, is a riddle to which no key has yet been found.   And how each partial self, and the whole range of selves can occur as experiences at all; how they can then be thought about and this thought about them in turn be thought about, *ad infinitum;* how the feeling of the self as the same self can perdure through the succession of fleeting, fragmentary, often antagonistic, selves—all this remains unexplained, except in a superficial way, by neurologist, psychologist, and psycho-analyst.   In the end, Hudson is right: "For what do we *know*—and what *do* we know—what do we *really* and *truly* know about what a friend of mine will insist on calling our 'insides'?   Meaning not our lights, and livers and other organs, but that part of us where the mysteries are."   We are children abroad in the night, and the lanterns we carry throw their beams but a little way.   Mystery? Mystery indeed.   The mystery that grows and deepens with insight.   But not artificial mystery; not the added darkness that comes from blowing out the feeble lights we have.

The attempt to define the self concretely has this great advantage: it lifts the momentous fact into relief that selves are not born but realized, made, created through the contacts of life. It is true that the individual comes into the world with an inheritance from victories and defeats in a struggle of uncountable centuries. He comes with a given body and a given stock of impulsive capacity. He cannot add a cubit to his stature, he can do little to change his looks, and he must manage to get on with the brain and the nervous system he was born with. He is, however, subject to another inheritance, a social inheritance, likewise reaching back through the ages, and this too is implicated in determining what he may become. That this social environment —education, institutions, customs—has *something* to do with the self is altogether too obvious to have escaped notice. The social medium of course provides a good or a poor opportunity for growth and development. But the truth goes far deeper. We are coming to see, thanks especially to John Dewey, that the self is the *integration*—literally, not figuratively—of organism and environment. As water is the novel result of the combination of two gases, as vision involves eyes, objects, and light, so the self is the active amalgamation of inborn potentialities and environmental forces, physical and social.

We may see this very clearly in the language we speak. The elemental vocalizations of the human offspring probably differ very little whether the birthplace be Baraboo or Borneo. Yet combined with the linguistic influences of the former place, the resulting speech is English, or, as some would say, American, while combined with the linguistic influences of the latter place, it is Dyak or Pulupetak. In the same way are produced the widely different conceptual worlds associated with these languages, and, indeed, the whole complex collection of interpenetrating habits of thought and feeling and action which constitutes the one self as contrasted with the other. For every individual must work up his share of impulsive life into effective ways of dealing with the world before him. And this calls for the intimate incorporation of organic processes and things outside. We cannot eat without eating *something;* we cannot *drive* a nail without driving a *nail;* and so we cannot think or feel or act in any way without bringing together, in a way analogous to chemical combination, the actor and the acted upon, or, as it were better to say, the acted *with.* If there were any advantage in doing so we might say that the environment forms habits when it gets organisms to form them with, instead of saying, as we now do, that organisms form habits when they get an environment to form them in.

The point can scarcely be emphasized too much.

If the acts of human beings involve the unification of propulsive activity and environmental means of expression, so that, as Dewey puts it, the latter has its say as well as the former; if these acts are the material of habits, and habits define the self; if this is so, it becomes of enormous importance to discover what may be ascribed to native endowment and what to the social medium. To this problem almost no attention has been given. Human nature, in all of its aspects, is thought of as *distinct from* its environment. We have either adopted from theology or theological metaphysics the notion that man has an "essential nature," or, if we made pretensions to being scientific, have taken from psychology or biology the equally one-sided notion that man is at bottom a larger or smaller collection of "instincts." In any case we fail to appreciate the fact that our so-called *human* nature is in many important respects *socially induced* nature. And disregarding this we uniformly counteract efforts made to elevate human motives by continuing in force the very activities, customs, and institutions which are mainly responsible for making them what they are. We deplore strife and bloodshed, but hold the instinct of pugnacity responsible, meanwhile strenuously resisting any attempt to alter the relations of life which make just such results inevitable. We blame the acquisitive instinct for our money madness, and the sexual instinct for our immoralities, yet meet every attempt to change the conception of property rights and sex propriety as a treacherous attack upon the foundations of civilized society. So in spite of all our teaching and preaching and struggling each new generation gradually grows to resemble the one that preceded it, not because each is an unfolding of an inborn, unalterable nature or a set of hard and fast instincts, but because the innate physical and mental energy of each new generation is received and molded into habits by the same environmental forces. Were these not complicated and contradictory, making a perfect incorporation of impulse and environment very difficult, not to say impossible, for sensitive spirits, civilized life would long ago have become utterly stagnant.

We may therefore conclude that the chief problem connected with the self has to do with the conditions under which the self develops. Granted that a limit is set by human nature on its side, this is a purely academic consideration unless we are utilizing, to somewhere near this limit, the powers that actually exist. Who can claim that we are? From childhood we are besieged with every inducement to make the accumulation of material goods the chief object of desire. To almost the same degree we are encouraged to shallowness of thinking and narrowness of sympathy. Naturally, then, this is the predominant type of self we meet. And the relatively small number who have sufficient fight in them to force their way to prominence are trained to be expert exploiters of their fellows. No doubt men had it in them to become what they became; nevertheless, out of the same original material a different social medium would have realized very different selves. A society which refused to identify life with business, which recognized business, as generally conceived, to be parasitic on life, and which recreated itself in response to this recognition, would liberate and develop human powers now left to atrophy or to find satisfaction in sentimentalism or dreaming. Dark as the present outlook seems, there are signs that a society, different in important respects, is not as impossible of realization as it was. We have already taken some steps in that direction. Those who follow us may move faster and with more confidence. If they do, men will become attached to new interests, a new spirit will live in human hearts, our heroes will be discoverers of social betterment, and with every social discovery a new opportunity will be opened for the realization of a nobler selfhood.

CHAPTER VII

SCIENCE AND THE HIGHER LIFE—THE RENEWAL OF WARFARE

ONE of the surprises of the last few years has been the reopening of the warfare between science and religion. Most people interested in either of these fields were, no doubt, more or less aware that antagonism of some sort existed, but few were prepared for the outbreak of militant hostility or "for the exchange of anathemas," as a leading periodical puts it, "between pulpit and laboratory and a mutual consigning to fire and brimstone reminiscent of the sixteenth century." Militant hostility between science and religion was thought to have ended once and for all with the victory of science in the last quarter of the nineteenth century. But that is the way with victory in war. It does not solve the problem out of which the conflict developed. In this respect there is nothing novel or unusual in the present flare-up of the old battle.

The more immediate occasion for the outbreak was the struggle with Germany; and first of all the recently aroused hatred of all things German. Was not Germany the most brutal and barbarous nation on earth and at the same time the most scientific? Who could fail to see the obvious connection? This view, widely held as we know, was spread out at length in an article entitled "Drift" in the *Atlantic Monthly*. Under the leadership of Germany, the argument there runs, we have been brought to worship science until "science has become a religious mania, and its fruits are like the fruits of a religious mania. The world is familiar with them. Torture, persecution, bloodshed, indiscriminate assassination and the sins of the spirit which are worse than real murder: pride and intolerance, burning hatred of all those who refuse to do obeisance to the fanatic's deity, and that last corruption which, seizing upon the soul of the fanatic, makes him see all human truth as one mass of lies, and all lies as truth." So the author strides on. An editorial in *The New Republic* aptly compressed the article into this simple formula: "The Germans are Science. Science is the Zeppelin. The Zeppelin is murder. Therefore, science is hell." While most Americans did not thus clearly formulate their convictions, yet in the backs of their heads an identification was often made between science and the enemy they abhorred, and the feelings entertained towards the latter spread to the former by a very familiar contagion.

The war brought science under suspicion in another way. Even while we were rejoicing at the
discovery by scientists of ways of thwarting our enemies and were hoping and working to invent means
of destruction more ingenious and powerful than
anything they might produce, the thought was often
present to our minds that this was after all a miserable business to put our best talents to. Such
thoughts were for the most part repressed at the
time, but not altogether, and not without having
their effect. Here and there a bolder spirit voiced
his fears of a scientific civilization, and scarcely had
the conflict ended when protests were heard from
all sides against the surrender of life to science.
Every year since then has intensified this feeling.

This is one side of the matter. On the other side
the war made impossible continued adherence to
former ideals. In an incredibly short time we witnessed the fall of dynasties that had come to seem
almost a part of the constitution of things. We saw
the expenditure of wealth and energy on a scale
never dreamed of before. We accomplished tasks
so huge that we could not antecedently have thought
of them, to say nothing of thought them possible.
We deliberately killed and wounded human beings
in such numbers and destroyed property in such
quantity that even natural catastrophes pale in com-

parison. Men cannot pass through an experience like that and quietly return to their former circle of ideas. They cannot go back to the philosophies and creeds and ideals out of which these experiences wrenched them.

And they did not go back. Peace, which was to set us well on the way toward the social and political millennium, plunged us instead into spiritual bankruptcy and into general despair of moral purpose. Many people, especially of the younger generation, suddenly freed from the restraint of customary inhibitions, locked arms with jazz and are gayly frolicking down the green valley of life. Many others, especially of the older generation, equally adrift but too feeble of will or too stiff of limb to adopt so light-hearted a method, have turned their backs upon the problem and have fled to some physical or mental retreat. A book like Sedgwick's recently published *Pro Vita Monastica,* recommending that men and women drown uneasiness in some bright illusion, wooed in semi-monastic retirement, is justly advertised as having met with immediate and wide response from the homesick of all creeds.

The published indictments that have grown out of this situation are often superficial diatribes whose source is ignorance and bigotry. There are, however, more serious, high-minded criticisms, and of this type an essay named "Whither," published anonymously, is representative. "In a final division of household possessions of my ancestors," says the writer, "a quaint gray chest has brought me a heritage of unexpected value in packages of letters, written many years ago and tossed carelessly here with mouse-eaten diplomas and articles of ancient wear. As I read, deciphering oftentimes with difficulty, the old-fashioned handwriting on the yellowing paper, I pause to marvel. What fullness of life is here! What richness! What greatness! . . . Written out of narrower lives, so far as mere worldly circumstances go, than those with which I come in contact to-day, they reveal a far deeper life, a profounder hope and faith, a recognition of wider horizons than most of our contemporary world knows. Here is a knowledge of spirit as the one great reality; of divine meanings everywhere; a sense of the greatness of the issues in life as a warfare waged in the name of the soul; faith in the undying character of righteousness, in the endlessness of human hope. Words are traced which take away one's breath, in the grandeur of their denial of what seems, in the splendor of assurance."

"Letters that I am privileged to see to-day," she continues (assuming "she" to be the correct pronoun), "are as different as if they were written by a different race; chance articles in newspapers and journals, intended to appeal to the contemporary public, reënforce the impression in regard to our present absorptions, our present limitations. These later letters are no less full of human tenderness, and possibly they are more outspoken in regard to it, but they bespeak an inner poverty, a contrasting narrowness of life. Their largeness, if wide horizons are suggested, is external, geographical—the largeness of travel abroad, by land or sea, of motortrips there or at home. They are full of restlessness, desire for change, rushing hither and yon. Their great concern is with material things: diet, dress, details of operations, fluctuations in stocks. . . . The horizon is near and attainable; the sky comes down like a brass bowl over our heads; I stifle in this world of nostrums, of remedies, of external cures for moral evils. This superficial material optimism which ignores the deepest need, the deepest answer, fails to suffice. One is aware of a lessening life, a drying of the very sources of vitality; the old sense of illimitable destiny, of greatness, of the challenge of eternity is gone."

The reason for this deplorable change is due, we are told, to a kind of materialistic Epicureanism which, under the leadership of Science, dominates

the modern world. "Robbed of Eternity, we mean
to make Time pay to the uttermost—hence this
nervous excitement, this feverish activity. . . . We
have but a few minutes in which to rob the house
of life; let us seize all the articles in sight; death,
the householder, is even now waiting to take us into
custody. . . . We will crowd all into the swift,
flitting minutes, though Life should break in the
process."

And what has been gained to recompense this
tragic loss? Nothing essential, thinks the writer.
"The human mind has suddenly been diverted by
a loud noise outside," that is all. "It is a noise of
motorboats, aeroplanes, engines of all kinds; a sight
of airships, flying like birds; of submarines, diving
like fish; of moving pictures with their endless
panorama. Mankind is childishly diverted; the
hearing of the ears, the seeing of the eyes—it is
enough." To be sure, "we hear endlessly of the
great advance of our time, of the surety of its
knowledge, the doing away with baseless old ideal-
isms. What, after all, has been achieved? The origin of human thought, the destination of the human thinkers, are as profound a secret as before
this unparalleled progress. Science, which has been
the great intellectual adventure of the last century
—to what has it led us? Only again to the edge of

the unknown, where we confront the infinite.   It
has not gained by one hair's breadth upon the en-
compassing mystery of our lives." When all our
boasted knowledge has been counted in, we must still
say, in the words of another writer:

"But beyond the bright searchlights of science,
    Out of sight of the windows of sense,
    Old riddles still bid us defiance,
    Old questions of why and whence.
    There fail all sure means of trial,
    There end all the pathways we've trod,
    Where man, by belief or denial,
    Is weaving the purpose of God."

In answer to such criticisms as this reflected in the
secular and religious press, scientists and religious
leaders in various parts of the country have declared
that no conflict actually exists.   "The fact is," says
a professor of zoölogy in one of the larger universities, "that with a proper understanding of terms,
science and religion, there not only has never been
but there cannot be a conflict between the two."
The president of one of the leading state universities, himself a scientist, writes: "I have never found
it necessary to justify religion to science or to excuse
science to religion.   I have accepted both as equally
divine revelations, and both as equally wrought into
the constitution of the world.   I have believed that

wisdom and might are God's and I have equally believed that science reveals to us how that might and that wisdom are expressed in the operation of the world." And as if to settle the matter by one bold gesture, a noted physicist formulated a document intended to show that according to leaders in science, religion, business and politics "it is a sublime conception of God which is furnished by science, and one wholly consonant with the highest ideals of religion." Forty religious leaders, scientists, and men of affairs signed his declaration beginning with these words:

"We, the undersigned, deeply regret that in recent controversies there has been a tendency to present science and religion as irreconcilable and antagonistic domains of thought, for in fact they meet distinct human needs, and in the rounding out of human life they supplement rather than displace or oppose each other."

In spite of these assurances (which are merely illustrative of statements issued from pulpits, laboratories, and editorial desks from one end of the country to the other) many people refuse to be convinced. And large numbers of them respond sympathetically to such essays as "Whither." They are convinced by the logic of these attacks upon science, and they agree that whatever interpretation we may give to the ultimate mystery, for a way of life we must go back to the faith which, under the influence of science, we have rejected. "Our forefathers tried and proved it and found it good, living difficult lives and dying hard deaths full of a sense of conquest, of triumph. Their working hypothesis has yet to be surpassed." That is the declaration in "Whither." Irving Babbitt expressed the idea in two sentences in *The Weekly Review*: "The Occident is at an *impasse*. There are signs that it is going to be forced, however unwillingly, to return to the truths of the inner life that it has discarded."

But if those who acquiesce with this demand analyze the situation a little more closely, their acquiescence may perhaps become less wholehearted. They may wonder whether they really care to go back to the discarded concept of life, however reinterpreted; and they may doubt the very possibility of going back. For, in the first place, they will perceive that under the spell of the quaint gray chest and the yellow letters the authoress of "Whither" has oversimplified the picture. "One is aware," she remarks in passing, "of certain immovable tenets of hard theology, but I note that these have small part in their thought." Isn't this tripping a little too lightly over a significant aspect of "the way in which faith vitalized their daily lives"? If one tries to recover a completer picture of those good old days one notes that "certain immovable tenets of hard theology" played a rather large and not always an admirable rôle in affairs. The redeeming feature of the situation was that then, as always, men were better than their creed. The hard theology was frequently softened in application because it was put into practice by human beings, beings with fellow-feeling, which no creed has yet been able to stifle altogether. But the fact that the human spirit was able to triumph over it does not justify us in disregarding or minimizing the weight of this theology as it rested upon human life. It gave men a cosmic outlook and a philosophy of life, such as they were; but it likewise invested unbelievable narrowness of spirit, the basest motives, the grossest impulses, the most refined cruelties with the sanctity of God's holy will.

Those who urge us to return to the faith of our forefathers are prone to forget that they view the theology of the past in the softer colors of its setting rather than in the light of its noonday glare. John Adams, writing in his old age to Thomas Jefferson, perhaps at the very time when the letters in the quaint gray chest were penned, was not so easily deceived. "God," he writes, "created this speck of dirt and the human species for his glory; and with the deliberate design of making nine-tenths of our species miserable forever for his glory.   This is the doctrine of Christian theologians, in general, ten to one.   Now, my friend, can prophecies or miracles convince you or me that infinite benevolence, wisdom, and power, created and preserved for a time innumerable millions, to make them miserable forever for his glory?   Wretch!   What is his glory? Is he ambitious?   Does he want promotion?   Is he vain, tickled with adulation, exulting and triumphing in his power and the sweetness of vengeance? Pardon me, my Maker, for these awful questions. My answer to them is always ready.   I believe no such things.   My adoration of the author of the universe is too profound and too sincere."

It would seem that the metaphor of "the sky coming down like a brass bowl over our heads" would fit the world-view from which John Adams, for one, was happy to have freed himself after years of struggle—the world view of our forefathers—better than it does anything that might be called a world-view to-day.   To a degree this is conceded by the defenders of the faith in question, for they assure us that it is not the older creed in its literalness which they champion.   Although they are the descendants of the stern and rugged old Puritans, as Randolph Bourne put it, "who wrestled with the devil and stripped their world of all that might seduce them from the awful service of God, they have succeeded in straining away by a long process all the repellent attitudes in the old philosophy of life." In that case what becomes of the logic of their position, since it was exactly these repellent attitudes which gave the faith of our forefathers its finality and authority, and since it is exactly this finality and authority they feel the need of?

There is a still more fundamental objection. Men simply do not go back to a philosophy of life that has once lost its vital grip upon them. To bring the Occident back "to the truths of the inner life that it has discarded" is as possible as to keep the sun down by sitting on the horizon. In certain periods of man's history a particular conception of his origin and destiny, and the consequent meaning and purpose of life, once adopted, remained practically unchanged for long stretches of time. Conditions responsible for this permanence, however, were undermined when men began seriously to inaugurate the Baconian program of interrogating Nature, with the purpose of its progressive mastery. Thenceforward, the conception of man's relation to the general scheme of things was modified to some extent from generation to generation by the advance of knowledge. The modification was by no means steady or uniform.   Intellectual habits are resistant to change as bodily habits are, and they are especially stubborn when they are generalized as customs or enshrined in institutions.   Changes in significant conceptions must make their way against this tendency of ideas to become fixed and sanctified.   Periodically the collected mass of these habitual and institutionalized ideas dams back the stream, so that only a fraction of the accumulating knowledge flows into the current of everyday life. Sooner or later, however, the dam begins to leak, imperceptibly at first, then more and more seriously, until finally it gives way altogether.   For a time there is chaos and confusion, but the flood subsides, the débris is cleared away, and life is reconstructed on a new level.

The present is a period of this kind.   For generations a new concept of the nature of the unity connecting the fragments of our finite experience had been developing without finding a free opportunity to function in man's thinking or acting.   The new concept found this unity in the material basis of experience, rather than in a spiritual being other than matter, and for this reason it was highly unacceptable.   The influences at work to make the new view prevail were everywhere opposed.   Sanctified customs and sanctified institutions held them back; held them back, however, less and less successfully with each generation. The conflict culminated in the battle over the theory of evolution and its gradual elaboration to cover the whole range of knowledge. With the victory of the evolutionists over their opponents in the last quarter of the nineteenth century a new world view became inevitable. The dam was already leaking badly when the world war and the far-reaching social experiment in Russia released the flood. Finding ourselves adrift, with our trusted landmarks slipping from us, it is natural that we should reach out for the old stability in the old places; natural too that we should vent our nervousness in fulminations against whatever or whomever we believe to be responsible for our plight. To no avail. We shall either begin the creation of a new philosophy of life, or, lacking the wisdom and the daring, leave the task to others; we shall not recover what was swept away in the flood. Unless we can fashion new spiritual values out of the material at hand, out of the impulses and aspirations, the emotional and mental powers of contemporary human beings, mankind must suffer the consequences of our spiritual collapse. We need not exaggerate these consequences, we need not assume that the destiny of mankind hangs upon the choice of the present generation, for the recuperatory powers of mankind have shown themselves to be extraordinary. They may be equal to the new emergency. Still there is just enough truth in a certain law of sowing and reaping to make spiritual reconstruction imperative just now, both for us and for those who shall follow us.

No refutation, however, of any specific criticism of science goes to the bottom of the matter, especially when the criticism is associated with a demand for the reinstatement of a particular form of religion. Below such specific attacks, motivating and vitalizing them, is the conviction that science and the life of the spirit are incompatible. A belief so persistently, deeply, and widely held cannot be utterly without contact with facts of some sort. Vigorous, even bitter controversy existing side by side with the reiterated assertion that there is really no occasion for difference, suggests ambiguity, the unrecognized presence of a significant difference of meaning. V. T. Thayer has put the situation with precision in these words: "We doubt whether any one who is genuinely troubled regarding the conflict between his religious beliefs and his conception of scientific conclusions will derive comfort from the public declaration of the forty scientists, statesmen, ecclesiastics, and business men denying the existence of a conflict between science and religion. Their statement takes for granted *one* interpretation of science and *one* type of religious attitude, and universalizes these. Such procedure remains blind to the living conflict which actually obtains in individual minds."

The fact of the matter is that the contemporary man is divided against himself. He is unwilling to forgo the practical results based upon the achievements of men of science, but he is fearful lest the development and application of scientific method shall deprive human endeavor of meaning and worth. The question is whether this state of mind is necessarily final. Are science and human values by their very nature incompatible, like God and Mammon, leaving us no choice but to serve the one or the other? Spiritual reconstruction leads through this question. And the question is so momentous that we ought to arrive at an unambiguous answer if that is possible. We can understand why men who are convinced that science must be developed at any cost may be anxious to allay public suspicion, especially at a time when the public is inclined to be obstreperous; and we can understand why other men who feel it to be supremely necessary to win thinking people to established religion may be willing just now to enter into an arrangement with science. But the problem reaches beyond these measures of practical expediency; beyond any will to believe. We need to be clear regarding the relationship between the values represented by scientific development and those represented by a vital higher life, in order that in aligning ourselves we may not betray the very interests we aim to safeguard. We must therefore go a little more deeply into the matter.

CHAPTER VIII

SCIENCE AND THE HIGHER LIFE—THE
ISSUE DEVELOPED

THERE can be no reasonable doubt that the thoughtful person's first contact with the scientific point of view is disquieting. It ushers him into a world of universal, rigid, inexorable law, indifferent alike to his laughter or his tears, and posits this as the *real* world. From the scientific point of view, our relations to the universe are, as Josiah Royce says, "relations to an essentially foreign power, which cares for our ideals as the stormy sea cares for the boat, and as the bacteria care for the human organism upon which they prey. If we ourselves, as products of nature, are sufficiently strong mechanisms, we may be able to win, while life lasts, many ideal goods. But just so, if the boat is well enough built, it may weather one or another passing storm. If the body is well knit, it may long remain immune to disease. Yet in the end the boat and the human body fail. And in no case, so this view asserts, does the real world essentially care for or help or encourage our ideals." For this reason most men and

174

women find the introduction to science a chilling experience—much as if they had entered a damp cav-
ern from a sun-flooded landscape.

And what of farther acquaintance with science?
Perhaps our thoughtful person reads the popular
essays dealing with scientific method and scientific
knowledge appearing in the newspapers and magazines. The outstanding propaganda of these deliverances is the need for a mechanistic conception of
life. "Let us consider every man and woman an
apparatus," is the plea; and let us study how to secure the desirable reactions from them. "If in an
apparatus we want to induce an electric current,"
says one of these popularizers, "we proceed to apply
the stimulus by mechanical means. If the current
does not generate we know there is something wrong
with the machine. Under the right conditions and
with the proper stimulus, a current is sure to be gen-
erated."

Exactly so with human beings. "Men and women
are machines, vastly complex, but operating under
definite laws; and the golden rule to a better understanding of them is to learn the nature of their
[physical-chemical] reactions." All that stands in
the way of a new dawn in art, literature, social relations, life in general, is our perversity, our obstinate
refusal to reduce every feature of life to a scientific

basis.   With science applied universally we shall be
able to secure the perfection of life with the direct-
ness and certainty of all mechanical processes.   We
shall secure good taste in art by inciting the proper
esthetic response, good will among men by arousing the sympathetic mechanism, intelligent behavior
by stimulating the judgment apparatus.   We shall
provide the requisite stimulus and get the inevitable
response, as we now get light by turning a switch.

There is a certain fascination about the scheme.
In the first place, it is simple, and simplicity exerts a
singular power over the human mind.   Then, too, it
appeals to the imagination.   One pictures the earth
conveniently covered with a population of perfect
human reactors, supplied, perhaps by wireless from
a central stimulating station, with the necessary
stimuli for all the needs and wants of life.   How
different from the present chaos, confusion, and
cross-purpose!   Yet somehow men turn from this
gigantic mechanical toy conception to something less
perfect but more human.   They are convinced,
whether they feel qualified to prove it or not, that
in such a universe not only is the material order indifferent to human values, but values in any vital
sense disappear.

And suppose our thoughtful person looks deeper.
Suppose he considers the two most conspicuous suc-

cesses of applied science, industry and war, what then? Undoubtedly the application of science to industry has accomplished marvels in the way of production and distribution, and consequently has added to man's physical well-being. It is a reiterated commonplace that all but the poorest men and women to-day enjoy physical comforts of which kings and queens were deprived a century or two ago. But scientific industry has cost a price. It has cost the enslavement of millions of human beings to a manner of life which renders the love of truth, of beauty, of goodness, all but impossible. Certain people are fond of retorting that the masses do not greatly miss these spiritual values. The retort is only partially true; and in so far as it is true it shows how wretched the state of the masses is. Appreciating this aspect of present-day industry many people have come to suspect that Samuel Butler was not joking but uttering a profound truth when he predicted the ultimate dominion of machines over men. I quote his prediction from *The Note Books:* "We take it that when the state of things shall have arrived which we have been above attempting to describe, man will have become to the machine what the horse and the dog are to man. . . . Day by day the machines are gaining ground upon us; day by day we are becoming more subservient to them;

more men are daily bound down as slaves to tend them, more men are daily devoting the energies of their whole lives to the development of mechanical life. The upshot is simply a question of time, but that the time will come when the machines will hold the real supremacy over the world and its inhabitants is what no person of a truly philosophic mind can for a moment question." Looking back over the past record of scientific industry or forward over the prospect, the man concerned for the life of the spirit can gather little hope. He does well if the survey does not cause him to lose hope altogether.

As to science and war, the situation is yet worse. We have just experienced the first real application of science to warfare, and the resulting destruction was so stupendous that it has not yet laid hold upon our imaginations. Moreover, it is common talk that the next war, because more scientific still, will be incomparably more devastating than the one just past. In the leading nations the best scientific genius is diverted, where possible, to the discovery of some means of bringing swift and utter destruction to the prospective foe, combatant and non-combatant, man, woman, and child. The last few years have given a new profundity to George Gissing's vision:

"I remember, as a lad, looking at complicated machinery with a shrinking uneasiness which, of course, I did not understand. I remember the sort of disturbed contemptuousness with which, in any time of 'examinations,' I dismissed 'science papers.' It is intelligible enough to me now, that unformed fear: the ground of my antipathy has grown clear enough. I hate and fear 'science' because of my conviction that, for long to come if not forever, it will be the remorseless enemy of mankind. I see it destroying all simplicity and gentleness of life, all beauty of the world; I see it restoring barbarism under the mask of civilization; I see it darkening men's minds and hardening their hearts; I see it bringing a time of vast conflicts, which will pale into insignificance 'the thousand wars of old,' and, as likely as not, will whelm all the laborious advances of mankind in blood-drenched chaos."

Facts like these are responsible for the prevalent impression of the spiritual ruthlessness of science. But is science really responsible? Is science to be held accountable for the superficial deliverances of zealous popularizers or for the generalizations of individual scientists who, looking up from their microscopes, test-tubes, measurements, formulas, construct the fullness of things in harmony with their professional bias? The answer is obvious.

So, too, with regard to the application of science

to life. The moral responsibility for the results of such application rests not upon science but upon the men who direct its employment. Science, like every other expression of human genius, lies open to the danger of exploitation; and the admitted spiritual devastation growing out of scientific industry and scientific warfare is the effect of this exploitation on a grand scale. Without science the steel industry would be impossible, but science is not to blame if 100,000 workers in the steel industry rise in the dark, work twelve hours, go home in the dark, isolated in the steel plants from family and nation. Science has made possible the building of a naval ship at a cost which would provide an increase of $800 a year for five years to the salaries of 13,000 school teachers, but science is not responsible for the fact that the money is put into naval expansion rather than into education. In these and a thousand other cases we must go back to the men who employ science as a means for attaining the ends they seek. In so far as the application of science to life has brought havoc to man's spiritual interests the responsibility rests upon those of our leaders who show no concern for these interests, and upon a public which persistently mistakes the savor of sentimentalism for the taste of spiritual reality, and, thus diverted, plays into the hands of the men who gamble for stakes involving the ruin of mankind. It will clarify the issue and abundantly reward the effort if we distinguish between science and the ambitions of men who, themselves not scientists, exploit science for ulterior ends.

It may be objected that this is after all a superficial appraisal of the facts. The very nature of science (we may be told) rules out considerations of value. From the scientific viewpoint there is neither good nor bad, noble nor base, beautiful nor ugly, desirable nor undesirable; for these are qualitative terms, and science deals with quantities, not qualities. No field of knowledge is recognized as a science until it is able to reduce its subject matter to a quantitative basis, so that as science has developed, the domain of quantity has everywhere encroached on that of quality. It follows that as life comes more and more under the influence of science, considerations of value must more and more disappear, until the whole hierarchy of them is reduced to the neutral level of quantity. The sophisticated man or woman will therefore even now recognize words designating qualities as "dear names men use to cheat despair," and will know that what they stand for are fantasies, due (as the ancients used to say) to a "twitching of the soul not in good health."

Consider this pronouncement, typical of science,

from a book by the late R. K. Duncan, Professor of Industrial Chemistry in the University of Kansas:

"We believe—we must believe, in this day—that everything in God's universe of world and stars is made of atoms, in quantities x, y or z respectively. Men and women, mice and elephants, the red belts of Jupiter and the rings of Saturn are one and all but ever shifting, ever varying swarms of atoms. Every mechanical work of earth, air, and water, every criminal act, every human deed of love and valor: what is it all, pray, but the relation of one swarm of atoms to another?

"Here, for example, is a swarm of atoms, vibrating, scintillant, martial—they call it a soldier— and, anon, some thousands of miles away upon the South African veldt, that swarm dissolves—dissolves forsooth, because of another little swarm— they call it lead.

"What a phantasmagoric dance it is, this dance of atoms! And what a task for the Master of Ceremonies. For mark you the mutabilities of things. These same atoms, maybe, or others like them, come together again, vibrating, clustering, interlocking, combining, and there results a woman, a flower, a blackbird or a locust, as the case may be. But to-morrow again the dance is ended and the atoms are far away; some of them are in the fever germs that broke up the dance; others are the green hair of the grave; and others are blown about the antipodes on the winds of the ocean. The mutability of things, and likewise the tears of things: for one thing after another,

> " 'Like snow upon the Desert's dusty Face
> Lighting a little hour or two—is gone,'

and the eternal, ever changing dance goes on.

"Now, whether we call the atoms God's little servants or the Devil's Agents, one thing is sure—that every action of every thing, living or dead, within this bourne of time and space, is the action of one swarm of atoms on another, for without them there is but empty void."

Atoms and empty void! What room is left in such a world for a life which has its source in the actuality of values? We may remain blind to this outcome by refusing to develop the view to its logical limit, but thus developed, values are utterly squeezed out. In such a world the wisdom of life is easily arrived at, and it was long ago expressed in the poem from which Professor Duncan quotes, though literal adherence to it, in America, is somewhat more difficult than formerly:

> "Come, fill the Cup, and in the fire of Spring
> Your Winter-garment of Repentance fling;
> The Bird of Time has but a little way
> To flutter—and the Bird is on the Wing."

Is this conception of reality as a blind dance of atoms the upshot of science? If so, does the atomistic standpoint of science carry with it the reduction of human life to a mechanistic basis?

A direct and clean-cut answer to this question is given by Jacques Loeb of the Rockefeller Foundation. Mr. Loeb discusses the question "whether our present knowledge gives us any hope that ultimately life, i.e., the sum of all life phenomena, can be unequivocally explained in physico-chemical terms." He argues that "if on the basis of a serious survey this question can be answered in the affirmative our social and ethical life will have to be put on a scientific basis and our rules of conduct must be brought into harmony with the results of scientific biology." And he believes that the question *can* be answered in the affirmative. The argument may be developed in this way:

Until recently doubt as to the real existence of molecules provided the anti-mechanists with a solid foundation. But this doubt has been removed. "We know to-day not only that the molecules exist, but we are able to state the exact number of molecules contained in one gram of a given substance." Thus we can state, with a possible error only in the decimal, the exact number of molecules in a gram of table salt or cane sugar. Since it has become possible actually to count molecules, "perhaps the greatest epoch in the history of the theory of cognition," physical science has been put for a long time, probably irrevocably, on a mechanistic basis. That is to say, "modern physics is mechanistic."

At this point the reader may be inclined to remark that life phenomena differ from those of physical nature. Yes, says Mr. Loeb; but not in a way to establish discontinuity between them. "The difference between the living and non-living consists not in the elements which constitute both kinds of bodies, but in the existence of specific structures and processes in the living which are not found in the non-living: for example, certain rhythmical processes, such as heart beat and respiration, which cease when the body dies, the phenomena of instinct and consciousness which no dead body shows, the phenomena of heredity, nothing analogous to which can be found in inanimate matter." This does not point to a difference in ultimate nature. It merely indicates that we do not yet see clearly how these phenomena may be reduced to the motions of electrons, atoms, or molecules. That the future will put this power within our reach is suggested by what is already known.

Observations on embryos of little marine fish (*Fundulus or minnow*), in which the heart is visible and where the heart beats can easily be counted under natural conditions, show that it is possible directly to trace essential life phenomena to the mechanistic concept of matter. For the laws of the velocity of chemical reactions (which are mechanistic) account also for the heart beats in the embryos of *Fundulus*. Other organisms, including human beings, differ only in the multiplicity of the conditions which influence the heart beat. If we can show that the rhythm of the heart beat conforms to mechanistic theory in one species where nature has prevented complications, why may we not assume mechanism where complications obtain which have thus far balked a similar demonstration? Or take the production by artificial fertilization of living young of organisms as complex as the frog—which has actually been accomplished; this also suggests that no discontinuity exists between the matter constituting living and non-living bodies. There is no longer any excuse for appealing to a mysterious "vital principle" to explain life processes.

Even more striking is the discovery of physical-chemical mechanism in the field of adaptation. "The astonishing harmony and adaptation of all parts in the body to the needs of the whole; the attraction of the male by the female and the provisions for the union of sperm and egg; the instincts of the fe-

male and occasionally of the male for the protection
and raising of the young; the instincts which guide
the young to their food, and many similar phenomena, are features without even a remote analogue
in inanimate nature. If the mechanistic method is
at all able to serve as a safe guide through the maze
of life phenomena, it has to stand the test of ex-
plaining adaptations."   That it does stand the test
Mr. Loeb illustrates by an observation made and
described by him years ago.

"A butterfly, *Porthesia chrysorrehoea,* lays its egg
upon a shrub. The larvæ hatch late in the fall and
hibernate in a nest on the shrub, as a rule not far
from the ground. As soon as the temperature
reaches a certain height, they leave the nest; under
natural conditions this happens in the spring when
the first leaves have begun to form on the shrub.
. . . After leaving the nest, they crawl directly
upward on the shrub where they find the leaves on
which they feed. If the caterpillars should move
down the shrub, they would starve, but this they
never do, always crawling upward to where they
find their food. What gives the caterpillar this
never failing certainty which saves its life, and for
which the human might envy the little larva? Is it
a dim recollection of experiences of former generations? It can be shown that it is the light reflected

from the sky which guides the animal upward. When we put these animals into a horizontal test tube in a room, they all crawl towards the window, or towards a lamp. The animal is, in biological language, positively heliotropic, comparable to the plants which bend their stems towards a window when raised in a room. It is this positive heliotropism which makes the animals move upward where they find their food, when the mild air of the spring calls them forth from their nest. . . . If we put these larvæ into closed test tubes which lie with their longitudinal axes at right angles to the window, they will all migrate to the window end and stay and starve there, even if we put their favorite leaves close behind them. They are slaves of the light.

"The few young leaves on top of a twig are quickly eaten by the caterpillar. The light which saved its life by making it creep upward where it finds food, would cause it to starve if the animal could not free itself from the bondage of positive heliotropism. The animal, after having eaten, is no longer a slave to the light, but can and does creep downward. It can be shown that a caterpillar, after having been fed, loses its positive heliotropism almost completely and permanently. If we submit unfed and fed caterpillars of the same nest in two different test tubes to the same artificial or natural source of light, the unfed will creep to the light and stay there until they die, while those that have eaten will pay little or no attention to the light. Their sensitiveness to light has disappeared; the animal after having eaten becomes independent of light and can creep in any direction. The restlessness which accompanies the condition of hunger makes the animal creep downward—which is the only direction open to it—where it finds new young leaves on which it can feed. The wonderful hereditary instinct, upon which the life of the animal depends, is its positive heliotropism in the unfed condition and its loss of this heliotropism after having eaten." Analysis shows that this heliotropism can be reduced to a simple physico-chemical law, namely Bunsen's and Roscoe's law of photo-chemical action, and so can be mechanistically interpreted. It would thus seem to be clear that eventually biology must follow physics.

Nor does mechanism end here. Everything generally included under the terms "psychic" or "the higher life" will in time be translatable into the same language. We have just seen that so-called adaptive instincts are in reality mechanistic processes. The next step is to show that the same is true of our mental and emotional life. "In spite of the gulf

which separates us to-day from such an aim," says
Mr. Loeb, "I believe that it is attainable. . . . As
long as a life phenomenon has not yet found a
physico-chemical explanation it usually appears inexplicable. If the veil is once lifted we are always
surprised that we did not guess from the first what
was behind it." So of the psychic, higher, or inner
life. "The contents of life," he suggests, "from the
cradle to the bier are wishes and hopes, efforts and
struggles, and unfortunately also disappointments
and suffering," and "our wishes and hopes, disappointments and sufferings have their source in instincts which are comparable to the light-instinct of
the heliotropic animals. The need of and the struggle for food, the sexual instinct with its poetry and
its chain of consequences, the maternal instincts with
the felicity and the suffering caused by them, the instinct of workmanship, and some other instincts are
the roots from which our inner life develops. For
some of these instincts the chemical basis is at least
sufficiently indicated to arouse the hope that their
analysis, from the mechanistic point of view, is only
a question of time." The conclusion is inevitable
that man's so-called mental and spiritual life must
permit of a mechanistic interpretation also.

It is true that a considerable number of scientists
refuse to subscribe to Mr. Loeb's generalizations.

Few scientists, however, would deny that the universalization of the mechanistic method is the trend and aim of science. What bearing does this have on the reality and significance of a higher life?

One of its manifest bearings is to render all such questions meaningless. If the term higher life is to have any significance it involves the assumption that a better or a worse state of affairs is actually possible and that man may deliberately be an agent in the production of the one or the other. Certain theories of universal inevitability, such as predestination and various types of oriental or occidental fatalism may leave room for a spiritual life through conceiving the determining power to be itself the highest form of ethical power, and through the derivative doctrine that man's higher life is a life lived in harmony with this ethical power. But mechanism differs radically from these theories. Mechanism reduces reality to a system of blind forces acting according to unalterable law, and it limits truth to results obtained by weighing and measuring in that system. Concepts of worth or value disappear or are reduced to chimeras.

This does not seem to be Mr. Loeb's conclusion. "If our existence," he asks, "is based on the play of blind forces and only a matter of chance; if we ourselves are only chemical mechanisms—how can there be an ethics for us?" Exactly. Here is a genuine difficulty, and it is met in a curious way. "The answer is," he replies, "that our instincts are the root of our ethics and that the instincts are just as hereditary as is the form of our body. We eat, drink, and reproduce not because mankind has reached an agreement that this is desirable, but because, machine-like, we are compelled to do so. We are active because we are compelled by processes in our central nervous systems; and as long as we are not economic slaves the instinct of successful work or workmanship determines the direction of our action. The mother loves and cares for her children, not because metaphysicians had the idea that this was desirable, but because the instinct of taking care of the young is inherited just as distinctly as the morphological characters of the female body." And so on.

Unfortunately this does not take us far. To argue that the higher life is compatible with universal mechanism because, being the outgrowth of instincts which are the reflection of inevitable mechanical processes, it is equally inevitable, does nothing to answer the question whether mechanism leaves anything but illusions for words like good, true, right, wrong, ought, and the like, to refer to. Unless by indirection it suggests that there *is* nothing else they refer to.

This bearing of mechanism is made clear if we remind ourselves that wherever the mechanistic explanation has been adopted as the ultimate truth it has driven out ethical concepts. Comets, earthquakes, lightning, disease, are familiar examples. Nor does Mr. Loeb shrink, in spite of what has just been cited, from coming to that conclusion. He is one of the thinkers, rare at any time but exceptionally rare in periods of intellectual flabbiness and confusion, of sentimentalism and passion, who do not cut their conclusions to conventional patterns. He does not make his views acceptable by clothing them in your favorite phrases. There they are in their scientific nakedness: take them or leave them, but do not ask that the truth be disguised to resemble your pet illusion.

So he tells us that mechanists welcome the news that John Hays Hammond, Jr., has invented a mechanical dog "which follows a lantern in the dark like the positively heliotropic caterpillar. The eyes of the 'dog' are of selenium, separated from each other by a wooden board which represents the nose, and allows one eye to receive light while the other is shaded. The electrical resistance of selenium is

altered by light; and when one selenium eye of the
'dog' is shaded, while the other is illuminated, the
electric energy which moves the wheels that take the
place of the normal dog's legs, no longer flows sym-
metrically to the wheels on both sides, and the dog
turns in the direction of and follows the lantern.
Here we have a model of the heliotropic animal,
whose purely mechanistic character is beyond question."

The implication of the illustration (as of the entire argument) is that human beings are in principle
identical with this clever device. And if the difference between a "heliotropic dog" and a human being
is solely one of relative complexity, we would seem
to be confronted with the alternative of admitting
the rationality of a possible higher life in the case of
the former or denying it in the case of the latter.
Confronted by this option there is but one choice.
Before making it, another position remains to be considered—that of the men of science who specifically
reject the conclusion thus far reached.

CHAPTER IX

SCIENCE AND THE HIGHER LIFE—LOOKING TOWARDS HARMONY

THE pass to which we have been brought is that science and the higher life are incompatible. If this conclusion is well founded there is nothing which could be more important for us to know and to face squarely. In certain quarters, as we have seen, the antagonism is declared to be entirely due to an unfortunate misunderstanding. Science and religion are said to be in perfect accord. This position has recently received considerable publicity in the daily press, in more serious periodicals, and in books. We must review this angle of the argument before we can claim to have examined the question.

One of the most interesting statements of this position, echoes of which have reverberated from many quarters since its publication, is that of the eminent biologist, J. Arthur Thomson, of Aberdeen University. "Our view," he writes in his *Introduction to Science*, "is that science and religion are incommensurables, that there is no true antithesis between them. Science aims to describe things as they

195

are and as they have been, and to discover the laws of all processes; it has definite methods of observation and experiment; it has its own 'universe of discourse' which does not include transcendental concepts and offers no ultimate explanations." Religion, on the other hand, "is evidently something altogether different from Science; it is beyond the tide-mark of everyday emotion and it is on the far side of intellectual curiosity." The language of religion "is not that of the street, nor of the studio, nor of the laboratory. And just as it is impossible to speak two languages at once, so it is a false antithesis to contrast science and religious interpretation,—they are incommensurable."

Nor can man find abiding satisfaction, according to Mr. Thomson, in the voices of Nature alone. "Invigorating, inspiring, and instructive they certainly are, but they are full of perplexities, and it is with a certain sad wistfulness that we hear their echoes dying away in the quietness of our minds like the calls of curlews on the moorland as they pass farther into the mist. Happy, then, in that quietness are those who have what Sir Thomas Browne called 'a glimpse of incomprehensibles, and thoughts of things which thoughts but tenderly touch.' "

Regarded in this way, the conflict does indeed seem to be purely imaginary. Science and Religion are independent, though complementary, reactions to the world; great thinkers, as he holds, representing "the aristocracy of the intellect," religious geniuses "the aristocracy of human emotions."   But a somewhat closer analysis reveals the fact that the position must be taken with a proviso, the proviso that religion be limited to pure feeling.   Religion and science are not incommensurable after all.   Religious feeling, Mr. Thomson explains, is usually associated with belief, and to some extent, though fortunately "to a continually decreasing extent, these beliefs touch the world of the concrete, and a clashing with science must arise whenever and wherever the form of the religious belief is inconsistent with the results of science."   Consequently there have been repeated clashes between the two because religious emotion had associated itself with concrete beliefs refuted by scientifically established facts.   As a result of these clashes "the particular 'body' which a religious idea takes, has been more and more sublimed."

Very naturally; and "sublimed" is just the right word, rich in emotional quality and free from specific meaning.   How much harsher such words as submerged, dissipated, or evaporated, would have been.   Harsher, but perhaps more accurate.   For what is the "body" of an idea but its meaning, its concrete references? And what is it to "sublime" this meaning but to evaporate or dissipate it? Mr. Thomson remarks that in most cases where the body of an idea has been sublimed "it has become clearer in the process." This he regards as the service which the so-called conflict between science and religion has done humanity. But there seems nothing for the word clearness to mean, as thus employed, except rarification into thin air.

For it must be added that Mr. Thomson does not make a well-known compromise; he does not permit the religious idea to nourish its "body" by drawing upon the vast unknown which hems in the small spot illuminated by science. He is too thoroughgoing and honest a scientist to suggest, as many do, that the unknown is incomparably greater than the known, and that there the soul may delight itself in fatness. On the contrary, he quotes with approval the words of Emil Boutroux, "The history of science proves that we have a right to affirm a continuity between what we know and what we do not know," and adds that the scientific enquirer has seen the solution of too many problems which our forefathers called insoluble to adopt transcendental explanations for unexplained events.

The conclusion of the matter would thus appear to be that religious emotion must refrain from for-

mulating itself in terms touching the field of knowledge, actual or possible.   And in that case the quotation "a glimpse of incomprehensibles, and thoughts
of things which thoughts but tenderly touch," is a
pretty phrase and nothing more.   Such words as
transcendental, "sublimed," incomprehensibles, and
the rest of the familiar vocabulary, have meaning
only on the supposition that science is not supreme
in the realm of the knowable.   The autonomy
granted to religion in the present instance is therefore a pseudo-autonomy, involving, as it does, belief
in nothing in particular.   Religion is assured of supremacy over a large domain providing it refrains
from taking the grant seriously and laying claim to
actual territory.   In the face of this qualification it
is difficult to agree that to see in the veto power of
science "an antithesis between scientific formulæ and
the religious idea is a misunderstanding."   On the
contrary, the conflict remains a very real one, in spite
of all denials.

Views in substantial agreement with Mr. Thomson's are widely prevalent among scientists in our
own country.   In contrast with the antagonistic or
neutral attitude of a few years ago we now witness
the most emphatic public endorsement of religion.
These endorsements come from all parts of the
country and from various branches of science, and

though they may differ somewhat in details they agree in substance of doctrine and in the admission of a degree of emotional flavor not commonly associated with science. The general features of this doctrine, suffused with this emotional flavor, are clearly presented in the statements by Robert A. Millikan, of the California Institute of Technology, who, incidentally, is one of the small number of physicists referred to by Mr. Loeb as responsible for laying a sure foundation for mechanism. And he presents the case in a way well adapted to examination. For these reasons, and because his utterances have had wider publicity than those of other scientists writing on the subject, he may with propriety be selected as representing the views of the American scientists who have felt called upon to justify science to the religious feelings of their fellow citizens.

"There seems to be at the present time," writes Mr. Millikan in *The Christian Century*, "a strange recrudescence of a point of view which is completely out of keeping with the developments of the age in which we live, a point of view which thoughtful leaders of both science and religion have in all ages realized never had any basis for existence." This view is the one under discussion, that science and religion are in conflict. He believes that the fact "altogether obvious and undisputed by thoughtful men is that there is actually no conflict whatever between science and religion when each is correctly understood." As a simple and convincing proof of this statement he adduces a list of notable scientists and religious leaders who have endorsed both. His argument is "that there can be no conflict between science and religion if the greatest minds in the two fields, the minds to which we look for our definitions of what both science and religion are, have not only not seen such a conflict but have clearly seen and clearly stated that there is none."

The conclusiveness of this demonstration may well be questioned. Disregarding other doubtful points, it is possible, to say the least, that the individuals cited, in spite of their eminence, have conformed to the common human practice of believing contradictory things; that they have never critically examined their dual allegiance, but have kept their scientific views and their religious views in separate idea-tight compartments. Until that possibility has been ruled out the proof is palpably weak.

But we need not follow this line of criticism farther, since the appeal to the authority of great names (a strange appeal to come from a man of science and which Bacon stressed as one of the idols which must be renounced at the very threshold of science) is not

depended upon to carry the whole burden of the
argument. A second fact is declared to be obvious
also, namely, that in the very nature of things there
can be no conflict between science and religion.
"This," according to Mr. Millikan, "appears at once
as soon as one attempts to define for himself what
is the place of science and what the place of religion
in human life. The purpose of science is to develop
without prejudice or preconception of any kind a
knowledge of the facts, the laws, and the processes
of nature. The even more important task of religion, on the other hand, is to develop the consciences,
the ideals, and the aspirations of mankind." And
the prospect becomes positively alluring if we look
at the relationship properly, as appears from these
words: "It is of course true that the scientific and
the religious sides of life often come into contact
and mutually support each other. Science without
religion obviously may become a curse, rather than
a blessing to mankind, but science dominated by the
spirit of religion is the key to progress and the hope
of the future. And history has shown that religion
without science breeds dogmatism, bigotry, persecution, religious wars and all the other disasters
which in the past have been heaped upon mankind
in the name of religion." True vision sees "science
and religion as twin sisters which are effectively

coöperating in leading the world on to better things."

So far, very good—perhaps too good. For were the facts really as simple as Mr. Millikan makes them appear, it would be difficult to account for what he himself calls "one of the most amazing phenomena of our times," the renewal of an estrangement between the twin sisters. The assertion that the estrangement has no real existence, when it is this very existence which calls forth the assertion, leaves something to be said. We must look for some explanation why, though there is no actual point of difference to separate them, the sisters show a strange disinclination to live together in harmony. And as we look, what do we find? We find that the trouble is one of mistaken identity. Each sister mistakes a crude impersonation for the other. No wonder they are in each other's hair.

Less figuratively, the point comes to this: science must be spiritualized, and religion refined. There is once more an implicit proviso. That is what is meant by the qualification, "when each is correctly understood." Let us make the proviso explicit. The science which is in harmony with religion is not that of the scientists "who lose sight of all spiritual values and therefore exert an influence upon youth which is unsettling, irreligious, and essentially immoral"; it is not materialistic science, "an altogether absurd and irrational philosophy . . . and so regarded by most thoughtful men." No, it is the science which "pictures God, however you may conceive Him, as essentially good, as providing a reason for existence and a motive for making the most of existence, and that we may be a part of the great plan of world progress." In the same way the religion which is in harmony with science is not the religion of the men of narrow vision who concern themselves with creed or medieval theology, but of those whose religion is "a life of service and the spread of the spirit of love," those who believe the essential function of the churches to be "stimulating us to right conduct, as each of us sees it, inspiring us to do as we know we ought to do, developing our ideals and our aspirations." The conflict is not between science and religion, correctly understood, but between true science and false religion, or false science and true religion.

But it is hardly safe to rest a conclusion of so much weight upon such slender props. The slightest touch of criticism makes the whole structure wobble, and a real push brings it down in a heap. For in the first place, it is by no means established (unless the words are taken in a loose sense) that science represents God "as revealing himself through countless ages in the development of the earth as an abode for man and in the age long inbreathing of life into its constituent matter, culminating in man with his spiritual nature and all his god-like powers." Not even what is referred to as "the objective evidence which the evolutionary history of the world offers" has been able to prove anything of the kind. The fact that, starting with the assumption of human supremacy, we can give a convincing account of how we arrived at the top, is by no means proof that a "determiner of destiny" exists, who has supervised the journey. The earth has indeed developed, life has evolved, and man, such as he is, has for the time being survived, but that leaves the issue quite open whether the process as a whole was aimed at or intended. This is not the place to argue so large a matter; it must be said, however, that a controversy which in one form or another has divided thinkers from at least the time of Democritus, and still divides them, cannot be settled by calm assurance and vigorous assertion vaguely put. And if it is not settled, one leg of the proof is gone.

Equally unstable is the other support. A little analysis shows that the advertised harmony involves stripping religion of content. The function of the church is stated to be "stimulating us to right conduct, as each of us sees it, inspiring us to do as we

know we ought to do, developing our ideals and aspirations." It is implied that men and women come
furnished with their own concepts of what is right,
ideal, and to be aspired to, and that the churches
generate the spiritual energy necessary to set them
going in the direction of their ideals. But we are
not left to implications. Mr. Millikan uses a metaphor which puts his meaning beyond doubt. The
church, he says, is to serve as "the great dynamo for
injecting into human society the sense of altruism, of
service, of brotherly love, of Christ-likeness."

It may be objected that figures of speech are to
be taken as embellishments of the argument, not as
part of its logic. On the contrary, a spontaneous
figure of speech, uncensored to make it conform to
what the author thinks he ought to say, is apt to give
the best picture of what he really believes. Mr.
Millikan is not concerned about the content or for-
mulation of the higher life. He specifically says
that its central concept, God, must remain vague and
indefinite, and that this makes no difference. Instead of "God" you may say "Nature," if you like,
or even "Something." And he refers to love, duty,
beauty, etc., as abstract conceptions. What religion
has to do is to make people *feel*—to make them experience a certain buoyancy and expansion of spirit;
to get them into the well-known keep-smiling, do-

for-others, things-are-worth-while attitude. And religion thus abstractly defined is (borrowing the phrase from William James) a blank cartridge. Noise and smoke, but no execution!

Now there are people who cannot accept this easy way out. They reject it for the same reason that they reject Mr. Thomson's more forthright position. Both withdraw attention from the greatest spiritual, or shall we say human, task of the times —the redefinition of the higher life in the hope of making it a function of man's effort to deal with the unprecedented social and economic conditions which, even if they are ignored, cannot be escaped. In their view, to stimulate, to inspire, to arouse, are not necessarily good acts. They are good if they aim at specific ends and these ends are good, but not otherwise. Experience has taught them a better psychology; has taught them that feelings reach out for objects as the tendrils of the grape seek the trellis or the hart panteth after the water brook. And so they know that to disregard creed—creed being the net result of thinking (in this case thinking about the higher life) expressed in a succinct statement of beliefs—is to wear one's heart on one's sleeve, a gift to any bold project that happens along, be it an honest enterprise or a clever exploitation. In their eyes sentimental goodness, and aspiration for its

own sake, are worse than worthless, because they not
only fail to meet the needs but constantly get in the
way of the application of thought to the problem of
defining the higher life in concrete, workable terms,
and the equally important problem of getting the
definition to take living form.

The issue is thus not of purely theoretical or logical interest. It is of great practical and social interest. In view of the current desire for intellectual
prestige on the part of religion and for moral respectability on the part of science any compromise
is likely to make a strong appeal. And in so far as
this particular compromise is adopted humanity surrenders two of its most signal achievements in the
realm of the spirit. The scientist jeopardizes his
dearly bought privilege of searching for the truth
regardless of its bearing on human hopes, and the
idealist gives up the long struggle to define his aims
and to justify his hopes at a time when these are
needed as never before. The adjective higher in
the term higher life is made synonymous with ob-
scurer, and the whole subject of ideals becomes a
phase of obscurantism. Peace on this basis is a
peace of diplomacy, which merely prepares the way
for intenser antagonism.

This appears to bring us once more to a stand.
Assuming that our analyses of the various typical

solutions of the problem in hand are correct, it would seem that nothing remains but for each side to fight for its claims, by any means available, until one or the other is forced to quit the contest. Before accepting this conclusion let us take a final look. Harmony both theoretical and practical may still be possible if instead of dealing with the problem on the surface we attempt to reach a more basic standpoint. Nothing is gained by decrying science, minimizing the importance of the higher life, or promoting a form of truce between the two which involves the surrender of what is most vital in each. Agreed on that much, we may be able to agree on more.

What is it men want? They want to live the most liveable life. This fact at once gives science a commanding status. The most liveable life must be sought and found in the physical environment which conditions our efforts and which, as far as we can see, is indifferent to our success or failure. Lacking acquaintance with this environment we cannot utilize it, and unless we can utilize it we are helpless. Rules of thumb, picked up by untrained observation, can take us some distance, and it is this which has served man from the beginning and still serves him in a thousand ways. Few people, however, even among the critics of science, would be willing to shrink life to dependence upon rules of thumb. They are not only willing to take advantage of the comforts and conveniences which a more refined observation has made possible, but expectantly await the more stupendous exploitations of nature which rumor constantly promises. Nature, then, is to be utilized. But to utilize nature, we must study nature, and scientific method is the best means so far discovered for that task.

But it gives the higher life a commanding status, too. Science, knowing no more of better or worse than nature does, cannot supply us with a program of life. And without that program science may be our undoing. This is frankly recognized by scientists themselves, or at any rate by the more thoughtful of them. The "results of Natural Science," says E. W. Hobson, in his recent Gifford Lectures, "in its persistent efforts to dominate physical nature, have furnished us with the mechanical means of securing an indefinite improvement in the welfare of mankind, if a wise use is made of the power with which they endow us. They have also provided our civilization with the material means of committing suicide, if the increased mechanical powers which they afford are not accompanied by a corresponding rise in the ethical standards which actuate nations in their dealings with one another."

Frederick Soddy has spoken to the same effect. Referring to the greatness of the as yet untapped atomic energy, and the efforts being made to discover a way of liberating it and applying it to useful ends, he says: "It is unlikely, but not impossible, that such a discovery might be made almost at once. A magnificent scientific achievement it would be, but all the same, I trust it will not be made until it is clearly understood what is involved. Let us suppose that it became possible to extract the energy, which now oozes out, so to speak, from radio-active materials over a period of thousands of millions of years, in as short a time as we pleased. From a pound weight of such substances one would get about as much energy as would be obtained by burning 150 tons of coal. How splendid! Or a pound weight could be made to do the work of 150 tons of dynamite. Ah! there's the rub. Imagine, if you can, what the present war would be like if such an explosive had actually been discovered instead of being still in the keeping of the future. Yet it is a discovery that conceivably might be made to-morrow, in time for its development and perfection for the use or destruction, let us say, of the next generation, and which, it is pretty certain, will be made by science sooner or later. Surely it will not need this last actual demonstration to convince the world that it is doomed, if it fools with the achievements of science as it has fooled too long in the past. Physical force, the slave of science, is it to be the master or the servant of men? The cold logic of science shows, without the possibility of escape, that this question if not faced now can have only one miserable end."

This conviction, that the so-called mastery of nature is in itself inadequate to the needs of life, is bound to become more deep and general as the conditions are appreciated. Indeed it may soon be the one, all-absorbing question of the age. We must therefore turn elsewhere for the complement of the great service which science has done and stands ready to do. And we must demand (or we shall fall back into positions already rejected) that this service, though different in important respects, must be of the same substantial kind we are accustomed to look for from science. We may, for example, study man's original impulsive equipment, his desires and habits, the purposes and cross-purposes which are formed out of these in response to physical and social conditions, and thus arrive at a conception of the best manner of individual and social life. Science would then be man's effort to master the facts of nature and to discover the best means for drawing upon nature's resources; and the higher life man's effort to master the problem of human values, or his devotion to the discovery and practice of the most liveable life. We might then indeed speak of science and religion, without equivocation or confusion, as inseparable and complementary endeavors in man's attempt to make himself at home on this planet.

Is such an arrangement feasible? Not without a radical change in the prevalent notion of both science and the higher life. Any genuine *rapprochement* implies the emancipation of the mind from the tradition that the one opens the window to ultimate truth and that the other comes armed with a supernatural warrant. No doubt reasons are forthcoming for holding to these traditional conceptions, but so long as each side clings to a sovereignty fatal to the other there must be discord between the two. A working understanding requires as an initial step a modification of time-honored claims. Without this step, harmony, however much advertised and eulogized, will be word-deep only. In the past this suggestion might properly have seemed hopeless, but there are reasons why it should not appear so now. Recent events have discouraged dogmatism and intolerance in both camps, and in its place there has developed a disposition to make concessions. At the same time the reports of profound changes in scientific conceptions, such as the electro-magnetic constitution of matter, the theory of relativity, etc., widely disseminated by newspapers and magazines, and the experience or observation of changing religious conceptions, have prepared the interested public for basic reinterpretations.

It remains to make clear then what this change in attitude concretely demands.   And while no change in the habitual outlook on the world could well be more revolutionary, a lengthy exposition is unnecessary to make clear the essentials.   The first of these is the recognition that scientific concepts and generalizations are not literal transcripts of reality but highly selective constructs of the human mind; not discoveries in the strict sense, but inventions, products of the creative imagination of men of genius. This fact has been adumbrated in various ways in the history of thought, and from different motives, but in recent times, especially very recent times, it has been clearly stated and defended from the side of science by Hobson, Mach, Ostwald, Pearson, Kirchoff, and men of like caliber.   Two citations will put the standpoint before us.

"Scientific method consists," says Karl Pearson, "in the careful and often laborious classification of facts, in the comparison of their relationships and sequences, and finally in the discovery by aid of the disciplined imagination of a brief statement or *formula*, which in a few words resumes a wide range of facts." It is these formulæ, according to Pearson, which are commonly referred to as *laws of nature*, and this leads to a very important problem, neglect of which, in his opinion, is the source of much confusion. The problem is, does a law of nature "really exist before man has given expression to it? Has the word any meaning when unassociated with the mind of man?" And he replies: "I hold that we must definitely answer 'no' to both these questions. A scientific law . . . is the *résumé* or *brief expression* of the relationships or conceptions, and exists only when formulated by man." For this reason he calls all great scientists, in a sense, great artists, and scientific laws the product of creative, disciplined imagination.

A similar view is presented by E. W. Hobson in the lectures already referred to. The term law of nature, he remarks, has too frequently been taken to imply an objective law which natural phenomena must of necessity obey, whereas it is in reality a conceptual law set up by the activity of the mind of man. It is not set up arbitrarily; it has an element of fact in it—the perceptual world from which it starts and to which it returns. But "Natural Science need not," in his view, "go beyond this recognition of the existence of this element of fact; it is unnecessary for its purposes to make the assumption that a single law has a precise correspondence with a single definite set of relations which actually subsist in Nature. Still less is it necessary for the purposes of Natural Science to assume that the law corresponds to a set of relations between real entities." The fact is, that "in all cases, the discovery, or rather the construction, of a scientific law involves that synthetic activity of thought which manifests itself in a constructive process in which actual percepts are employed only as the raw material and starting point of the mental process. In the attempt to discover a scientific law, a selective process is requisite in regard to the percepts, some greater or lesser part of what is perceived must be ignored, as irrelevant to the purpose on hand; this selective procedure amounts to a process of abstraction, in which some elements of our actual percepts are removed, and not attended to." And again: "A scientific law is accordingly always, in some greater or lesser degree, abstract, in the sense that it represents only a part of what is in any individual case actually perceived; it describes a particular sequence of physical events which, in an actual case, is accompanied by other percepts or events in relation to which the law has no application." And he points out that as a science develops to higher stages it becomes more and more abstract, until to the symbolic conceptions which have been derived by selective abstraction from the perceptual world, are added conceptions which have absolutely no counterpart in reality; which are formed by a process of constructive imagination to complete the conceptual scheme or to make it self-consistent.

This position is not accepted by all scientists, but it does represent a strong tendency, and it has a future. We need not, however, argue the question of its validity. Our object is merely to see on what view of science a genuine higher life is possible. And it would seem that it must be some such view as this. For if science is a great conceptual system arrived at by abstracting certain aspects of living experience and neglecting others, a symbolic picture woven into the garment of nature behind which, as Heraclitus said, she ever loves to hide; and if by means of this creation we are able to gain ends that appeal to us; two results follow that are essential to the higher life. One of these is a new freedom, freedom from an attitude toward conclusions in natural science analogous to the medievalist's attitude toward conclusions in scholastic theology. What ground is there for believing a divinity to hedge about a scientist, or for assuming that scientific con-

clusions, unlike other things human, are free from
the taint of imperfection and mortality?   It is important to insist upon the indispensableness of un-
trammeled science, but equally important to insist
with Clerk-Maxwell, himself an eminent physicist,
that "there are many things in heaven and earth,
which, by the selection required for the application
of scientific methods, have been excluded from our
philosophy" when we envisage the world with the
eye of science.

Which brings us to the second thing gained.   The
conceptual view of science not only leaves the way
open for, but positively suggests the necessity of,
other conceptual schemes for dealing with other aspects of life.   There is no longer any reason why the
principles or forms or categories under which the
scientist finds it convenient to think, *must* be employed by *every* thinker, no matter what his field or
his aim.   In our commendable desire to emulate scientific method we have become more and more obsessed with the notion that no matter what mutila-
tions or distortions might be necessary, everything
must be studied as we study chemical reactions or
falling bodies.   Differences in subject matter might
increase our difficulties but must not deviate us from
this procedure.   And this has been a costly error—
how costly there is no way of telling.   We do in-

deed want disciplined intelligence in every field, but disciplined intelligence is not necessarily identical with the specialized form it has taken in the physical sciences. This step—the clean-cut recognition that facts determine method, not method facts, that science is for life, not life for science—is of the greatest significance. It stresses rather than ignores the importance of appreciating differences in subject matter in order that the methodological procedure may be adapted to the nature of the problem.

The theory that men are machines may serve as an illustration. This theory is arrived at by abstracting certain aspects of human behavior and letting these symbolize the whole. When this partial view is applied in a circumscribed field not only is there no harm done, but it may prove highly beneficial in various ways; but when, its limitations lost sight of, it becomes the basis of great economic, social and political programs, the damage done is enormous. Unquestionably there are many actions of human beings which are machine-like. There are others which unquestionably are not. It is plain, for instance, that in contrast with other machines man's operations react upon himself and transform the nature of his operations, that is, make him a different machine. The change introduced may be great or small, but it is real, so that in the course of years the sum of the activities which make up a man's daily life may be quite decidedly altered. If we could point to typewriters which had gradually acquired the powers of linotype machines, and had then gone on until they functioned as rotary presses we would have a true similarity. A typewriter, however, might set up the entire Encyclopedia Britannica and, except for wear and tear, be the very same machine it was at the beginning. A typist, on the other hand, could not do this if she tried. True machines do not learn, while animals, and especially human animals, invariably do; true machines are the very symbols of uniformity and routine, while human beings are fundamentally antagonistic to doing the same thing over and over in exactly the same way. We can and do compel an approximation to machine-like behavior, but it goes against the grain, works only temporarily, and periodically leads to violent eruptions. It is difficult to see how this difference—a difference profound enough to be the chief cause of man's supremacy on the globe—can logically be disregarded.

This consideration is enforced by a second. Man evaluates or criticizes his experiences and processes, and he regrets, hopes, fears, craves, lays plans in consequence. Obviously, mechanical contrivances do nothing of the kind. A Ford does not aspire

to be a Marmon; an ocean liner may tower above
a tug but does not look down upon it. Where, outside of Kipling, do freight cars pine to be in Kansas
when the sunflowers bloom? To be sure, no one
supposes such things, but it is well to fasten our
attention upon this difference between true machines
and human machines long enough to guard against
being imposed upon by a common manner of speech.
Even in the animal kingdom we get hints of a kind
of selective adjustment to the environment which
differs from the wearing down adjustment of pure
machines. And what is present in animal behavior
in a very rudimentary form is highly developed in
human behavior. Men consciously select certain aspects of their environment and act with deliberate
reference to these aspects. They pass judgments
of value upon themselves, other men, and things,
and with these as guides, form plans of action aiming at the realization of particular goods and the
avoidance of particular evils; plans which may be
simple, and near in their attainment, or as comprehensive and far off as a philosophy of life.

A promising alternative is opened out when the
changed attitude referred to has become a living
thing. Instead of quietly ignoring these features
of human behavior or going to any length of twist-
ing and warping to force them into the conceptual

scheme adapted to the behavior of atoms and molecules, we may develop other conceptual schemes more hospitable to the facts, and so doing, may give a new purpose and consequence to the study of these processes. We put ourselves in the way of gaining ends to be reached neither by blind adherence to nor blind rejection of the highest specialization of human intelligence which science undoubtedly is.

At the same time the man in whom this change has become a living fact will find it impossible to reduce the higher life to conventional religion or to some form of trance induced by sitting on a peak of mystical abstraction gazing into the face of a oneness that is everything though nothing. He will rather identify it with active concern for the most liveable, joyous common life; with *dedication to the human venture*. He will not look upon the life of the spirit as a matter of revelation or immediate intuition delivered once for all to certain holy or wise men, and then forever striven after, but a life progressively discovered and progressively achieved by dedicated souls. He will endeavor to employ in his own way the disciplined intelligence best exemplified by the scientist; that is, he will try to conform to what may be termed the moral attributes of the scientific attitude: loyalty to fact, insistence upon rigorous, non-subjective standards of evidence, faith in the unbounded possibilities of coöperative achievement.   In that high sense he will be scientific. And he will agree with William James, that what most men need "is that their faiths should be broken up and ventilated, that the northwest wind of science should get into them and blow their sickliness and barbarism away."   But he will not make reality as pictured by natural science the model for human life.   He will not reduce to nothingness the attributes which in the course of evolution have distinguished man from the animals, nor will he aim to submit human destiny to the blinder processes of his own nature.   He will free life where he can from the sodden routine, the meaningless rush and scramble and defeat to which machine philosophy has already degraded it.   He will set his face against the conception of life where every knee shall bow and every tongue confess the Great God Hum.   Below all theories and creeds and faiths he will hold to the conviction that neither science nor religion nor art nor commerce nor any of the specialized forms of human activity is the end of man's endeavor, but a satisfying life for all who may have a life to live.

CHAPTER X

THE SOUL

THERE are two ways of taking the present world-wide agitation. We may take it negatively, as an evidence of disintegration, or positively, as a search for new meanings. This applies to the concept soul. Regarded in one way, soul is in process of losing all meaning; looked at in another, it is in process of gaining new significance.

Soul, as a word of common speech, came into use at a time when the western world had lost faith in the possibility of making anything of life. But the lure of life is difficult for men to resist. Preachers of world denial have never failed of followers, have had them sometimes in great numbers, yet life has always reasserted itself. So in this instance. For a time other-worldliness threatened to triumph over the love of life as it had over the fear of death. Christianity, however, increased in numbers. As it did so it naturally paid the price in various compromises, and among them this, that the religious life was no longer made synonymous with world-denial. Gradually men's aspiration after the higher life was again satisfied without the surrender of interest in secular occupations and contacts.

Indeed, after a few centuries, the original brotherhood of those who sought to flee earthly entanglements had grown into a rich, powerful organization which aimed to dominate rather than to despise the world. In spite of this drift toward secularization the other-worldly bias remained alive in at least two forms. Long after it had become a matter of course for the Christian to divide his allegiance between this world and the world to come, it was thought necessary for men and women who wished to live the religious life in its purity to retire to some retreat. By taking the vows of poverty, chastity, and obedience, that is by turning their backs upon the chief desires of the natural man, property, family, and power, they were thought to illustrate the *vita religiosa* in its highest form. Nor were the unsequestered freed from this influence. Even for them the higher life continued to be regarded as an episode in the fortunes of a soul whose real career was transcendental, and morality continued to be dependent upon a supernatural system of rewards and punishments.

In this dual form—emphasis upon the here and now, mindfulness of the hereafter—our religious

tradition speaks from below the level of consciousness to contemporary men. The ambiguity is height-
ened by the equivocal message of many of the spiritual leaders who would redefine the higher life to
meet existing conditions. Nothing is farther from
their intention, they tell us, than insistence upon
creed or dogma. That was all well enough for our
fathers, but we have learned that the important
thing is not what a man believes but how he lives.
Life! life! that is the important thing! Any kind
of life? No; of course not any kind of life. It
must be a certain kind of life; *the* life; life according to . . . and here the creed which was os-
tentatiously bowed out is quietly ushered in again.

The fact is that life on earth has regained its
place as the paramount interest of man, while the
conviction persists that spiritual values are by nature
foreign to this world and must be imported from
beyond. Hence the dilemma which confronts the
churches and the church organizations that seek to
keep in close touch with the conditions under which
their members live. It seems that the higher life
must take its character from these conditions but
also conform to the supernatural requirements. So
we have the growing emphasis on the need of a religion having direct reference to social, economic,
and moral conditions on earth, and the equally em-

phatic insistence that its motive power and its
authority must be supernatural.

Another factor enters for the generation that
has grown up in the prevailing scientific atmosphere.
Until the other day we still thought of the soul
as a substance, a thing-like essence resident within
and separable from the body, of superior, more persistent reality, and of higher destiny. It was to be
guarded from earthly contamination at any cost until liberated at death to enter upon its eternal career.
This concept, presented to men by Plotinus, whose
influence did much to shape the theology of the
early church and thus the religious life of the West,
is well indicated in this passage from his essay on
Beauty:

"If a man have fallen into filth or mud, whatsoever grace he had ceases to appear, and he shows
only as the thing the filth or mud has smeared him
into; ugliness has come to him by the accretion of
foreign matter; and if he is to be comely again
it must be his business to wash and clean himself
till he become what he was.

"So, we may justly say, a soul becomes ugly—
by an accretion, by an admixture, by a descent into
body, into matter. And this is the disgrace of the
soul, that it cease to be clean and apart. The disgrace of gold is in its being permeated with earthly
matter; if this be worked out the gold is left and

is beautiful—isolated from all that is other than itself, gold with gold alone. And so the soul; let it but be cleaned of the desires that come by its too intimate commerce with the body, emancipated from all the passions, purged from all that has accrued by its embodiment, withdrawn, a solitary, to itself again—in that moment the ugliness, that came only from the alien nature, is stripped away."

Immanuel Kant undermined this conception for philosophers a long time ago, without, however, greatly affecting its hold upon men and women in general. But the spread of biological and psychological ideas during the last fifty, and especially the last twenty-five years, has wrought a vast change. To-day not only the orthodox conception of soul but the very existence of soul is in doubt. William James, arguing against the existence of consciousness, quietly refers to "the faint rumor left behind by the disappearing 'soul' upon the air of philosophy." And though he does not speak for every one, since here again conflicting influences live in us side by side, there can be little doubt that the older ghost-soul has become generally unacceptable.

A widely prevalent attitude (which rarely gets into print) is bluntly voiced by Katherine Mansfield's *Raoul Duquette:* "I don't believe in the human soul. I never have. I believe that people are like portmanteaux—packed with certain things, started going, thrown about, tossed away, dumped down, lost and found, half emptied suddenly, or squeezed fatter than ever, until the Ultimate Porter swings them on the Ultimate Train and away they rattle." So saying he was doubtless more radical than the general opinion on the subject, yet the current conviction among the actively thoughtful leans decidedly in that direction. This is suggested by representative answers (of many hundreds) secured from college juniors and seniors to the question, Have you a soul? Two are by young men, two by young women:

"Have I a soul? Not in any sense of the word that I know anything about. Why? Because I have no empirical evidence for it, and, what is more important, because I'm better satisfied without one. A 'soul' almost necessarily implies immortality, and immortality involves the whole bundle of cruelties and superstitions I'm much happier without."

"Yes, indeed, I have a soul. It is not, however, the thing-kind of a soul I was taught to believe in. I really haven't any idea what it is. I know that it is sometimes big and overpowering, and that at other times it seems almost to leave me. I feel it most when I rise above life's sordidness and meanness and follow my better impulses. How to define it I don't know; but it is the best part of me."

"I have never worried much over the soul. When a high school course in physiology took away the idea that it was a physical something resembling a toy balloon and reposing somewhere beneath my ribs, it gave me nothing to take its place, and the word to-day has little meaning for me. I believe I can get along very well without it."

"My soul, I believe, is that part of me which embodies what is called one's conscience. It gives me my code of ethics. To others my soul is shown by my actions in various situations and circumstances. To myself it is somewhat different, in that many acts are misunderstood or misinterpreted and because my will doesn't always obey my soul."

These answers illustrate the growing tendency of western thought. By many the soul is rejected outright. By others it is believed to be something so vague and hazy that it is on the verge of passing out of existence. By still others it is made synonymous with moral sentiment or conscience. And if to such considered statements we add the creeds men publish in their unguarded utterances and practical activities we may conclude that, in spite of some evidence to the contrary, the western world no longer believes in the soul which once was the central concept of life.

This is significant as a mere matter of cultural

history. Its chief import, however, lies in its bearing on the world as a possibility, not on the world as a fact. For it marks a turning point in man's search for the higher life. In spite of variety of definition or no definition the concept soul has represented through the centuries an attempt to register a vital human experience and to express a deep human hope. The experience and the hope remain, though the traditional symbol may have lost its authority. Some people, in spite of everything, will doubtless cling to the older belief, even if they must make it meaningless through compromise. The majority will choose other alternatives. They will either press on regardless of the values represented by the outgrown symbol, or will find some way to give the symbol new meaning. A re-definition of soul, in the light of the contemporary emphasis upon the earthly life, and for those who cannot accept the traditional definition, is therefore in place. Let us attempt such a re-definition. Let us ask whether it makes sense to speak of soul in earthly, temporal terms, and, if so, what it may mean?

The moment the question is put in this form an answer begins to appear. It means, first of all, to have a part in the great spiritual assets which the human race has accumulated in its century-long effort to rise above the immediately given world of fact. One of these assets is literature. Books not only present pictures of imaginary times and places and peoples which may stimulate and guide to the attainment of a better state of actual affairs; they not only lead us into the presence of objects delightful in themselves; they do this, but they do more. They admit us into new worlds of direct experience and thus expand our mental and emotional horizons. Who that reads has not carried the spell of a book about with him for days, walking in the everyday world as in a dream? Who has not experienced the resulting emptiness when the spell was broken and the environment contracted to its habitual horizons? Practical life demands increasing concentration upon and preoccupation with material details. Busy about these many things men more and more neglect the thing most needful. Endlessly occupied they are prevented from considering the purpose of occupation. In this way thousands of people, both great and small, gradually lose contact with one of the great spiritualizing forces of life. For humanity so situated poets and authors do a two-fold service; they break the secular fetters and deck the firmament with shining worlds that the spirit of man may not utterly lose the way in the night called civilization. "There is a difference," said Emerson, "between one and another hour of life in their authority and subsequent effect"; and we may add that the hours spent in pilgrimages through the portals opened by books are of those that add a spiritual quality to a man's life.

Another of these assets is the tradition of beauty. If we trace back human ancestry as far as this can be done, the impulse to decorate or ornament is actively present from the start. Out of this rude, spontaneous beginning grew the desire to find and create beauty. Gradually the various arts developed, art products were accumulated and treasured, a new capacity to appreciate beauty in nature was born, a conscious purpose took shape to add beauty to the environment of everyday life. By imaginative participation in this process a man may free himself from the weight of the conventional atmosphere with its ugliness, squalor, and hardness of heart. Therefore to be familiar with works of art, to enter with sympathetic understanding into the function of the artist, to lose one's native blindness and see with the artist's eyes, is to acquire soul.

So of music. Comparatively few people are themselves musicians or know anything of the theory of music, but few do not know, with the sure knowledge of experience, that music has power to awaken the deeper levels of imagination, aspiration, and

will, and thus to break the tyranny of the petty logic
and the petty fact which tend to keep men on the
low level of ordinary existence. Consider an extract
from a letter to *The Freeman* describing one of the
last concerts conducted by Nikisch. Who can fail
to see in such experiences great moments in soul
biography? "The somber beginning of Strauss's
'Tod und Verklärung,' which closed the concert,"
it reads, "affected the German audience deeply.
They were hearing a glorious mass for their dead
millions. Nikisch, too, seemed moved. There was,
now, no hint of ostentation—not even an orchestral
'effect.' Terrifying was the struggle with Death;
terrible was Death's victory. Then out of the hollow subterranean music of winds and basses rose the
Transfiguration. With noble gesture and ineffable
serenity Nikisch piloted his theme above the earth,
above the clouds, through the seven heavens—and
left it shimmering in Eternity. There was no ap-
plause. The vast audience left silently."

But the spiritual assets accumulated by the human
race are not limited to the domain of art. For many
centuries man has struggled to free himself from
bondage to superstition, has acquired an interest in
objective truth and developed a technique for its
discovery and application. For many centuries, also,
man has conducted experiments in living, in the

course of which he has attained to great concepts
of life. No doubt contented lives are possible without the least awareness of either of these great
achievements, to say nothing of active interest in
the advancement of them, else the vast majority
of people would be dejected and miserable. To
be without this awareness, however, is to live deprived of the vision and the range of interests which
such awareness affords.

If we touch lightly upon science and philosophy
it is not because they are relatively less important,
but that we may concentrate upon the feeling of
human solidarity. In spite of obstacles and inter-
ruptions the recognition has continued to grow of
the interdependence of the various national and racial divisions of mankind. The term heathen is
practically obsolete, the term foreigner has lost its
edge, and the number of people who think and
feel in world terms is steadily increasing. The
familiar map showing a network of telephone wires
spreading like a great nervous system over the body
of our country, sending some vibration of its throb-
bing life to the remotest hamlet, is symbolic of all
sorts of other ways in which the people of the world
are bound together. Railroads and ocean routes,
postal and consular systems, trade and banking enterprises, news-gathering agencies, scientific, educa-

tional, and religious associations, and, latterly, the ubiquitous radio are a few of the obvious means of binding men into actually functioning types of union.

Now some people not only make use of these as conveniences, but sense their deeper significance. They recognize them as factors of human interdependence. And some, going deeper still, experience in themselves that more intimate bond which these practical ties can at best only further. They perceive that men are bound together by a comman human nature; that they go back to a common origin, are engaged in a common enterprise, are destined to a common defeat. Out of such appreciation grows an immensely greater kindliness and mutual appreciation. The man or woman who has attained to this elasticity of the emotions and the intellect which makes possible sympathetic appraisal of alien views and customs, of different national and racial contributions to the color and joy of life, has acquired one of the rarer expressions of soul. Daily duties and occupations, nearer ties and simple satisfactions have a genuine worth and importance of their own, and no life is laudable which spurns or lightly disregards them. At the same time a unique quality of soul is his whose spirit wanders afar though his body be confined to a few acres of land or a few miles of street, and who, while he does his day's

work with efficiency and neighborliness, is not ob-
livious to the larger adventure of which he forms
a part.

In these and similar ways men and women may
participate in spiritual race heritage and attain to a
richness of personality, a largeness of outlook, and
a sympathetic detachment which mark the possession
of soul. But soul may also mean to have a part
(though not necessarily a prominent part) in the
great human issues of one's time. These issues are
various, and some of them, such as those growing
out of the increasing self-consciousness of women,
the concentration of irresponsible economic power,
the militancy of the laboring class, the application
of science to war, the disintegration of religious
authority, will readily occur to mind. Outranking
them all, however, because underlying them all, is
the issue created by the prevalent concept of human
nature.

In their daily lives few people accept things as
they come. They do not accept any job, salary,
food, clothing, shelter, friend, wife, husband, that
may be presented to them and therewith remain
satisfied. They try deliberately to choose their lot,
and often show astonishing energy, ingenuity, even
heroism in the endeavor. In fact one of the more
obvious of human traits is the refusal to surrender

the hope of improvement in personal fortunes. The same people, however, lose this faith when contemplating social life. In place of a spirit of improvableness they hold to the conviction that the essential structure of society is unchangeable. Their reason is that the basal human motives (which social problems force them to consider) cannot be altered. Human nature is believed to be a changeless essence underlying men's conventional habits, a sort of living spring whence issue the impulses and desires that are perpetually manifesting themselves in conduct— a muddy spring, whose bubbling flow must be filtered through code or creed or dogma if life is not to be utterly defiled. And all such filterings leave the source untouched; they merely thwart, deflect, or conceal its free manifestation.

This conception of human nature as an active, wicked, unalterable essence walks with us in the street, works with us in shop or office, kneels with us in worship. It is the major premise of orthodox social, political, educational, and religious theory.

Where there is orthodoxy, there is heresy; that is to say, there are pioneers of a new vision. The very time that has witnessed the extension and intensification of this general belief in human impotence and depravity has also witnessed the growing expansion of a movement pitted against this view, a movement aiming to show, not by argument but by practical demonstration, that man's nature is not an essence which discloses itself willy-nilly when the time comes, but a center of propulsive energy, more or less organized in response to physical and social environment as habits of feeling, thinking, and doing. "For it depends on circumstances," as John Morley long ago said, "which of the chances that slumber within us shall awake, and which shall fall unroused with us into the darkness." The great task is the progressive discovery and creation of those circumstances which will enlist man's powers in the interest of the best attainable human nature. If the men and women dedicated to this venture in the business world, in social work, in the wide field of education succeed in arousing the interest of the average citizen in this movement; if they succeed in getting him to see that human nature is not something fixed and given, but something mutable and acquired, not something hidden away in human bodies ready to bubble over, but something created out of original capacity and environmental stimuli; if the average citizen can be brought to see this truth and to apply it, he will be enlisted in the greatest movement of our time, and will help to inaugurate a spiritual renaissance outranging in social significance any that has preceded it. Just as the rejection of the essence doctrine as regards physical nature, and the substitution for it of experimental interrogation, led to marvelous material results, so the free, inventive interrogation of human nature is sure of great social rewards. And what can be more natural than that in the effort to further the higher life of all the individual should further his own better possibilities?

There is a third and nearer way to the winning of soul. As things are, the tyranny of practical demands, the pressure of mass opinion, the fear of changes in social customs, and other less obvious influences cause most men and women to render only a theoretic or spasmodic loyalty to the higher life. It would be a deep-going transformation of personality if these men and women were to become, in their more local environment, their homes and communities, enthusiastic pioneers in the living, concrete application of the moral and spiritual aspirations of their time. In every home and hamlet and town the higher life is daily put in jeopardy. In every community from Gopher Prairie to Greenwich Village is staged a local dramatization of the conflicting tendencies that characterize the age. A man gains and nurtures soul as he participates in the effort to resist the insidious drift towards complete secularization that threatens modern life. He grows in spiritual stature as he helps to translate into family and community habit the best social vision of his day. No doubt the conflict wears a different face in different communities, but everywhere just now certain problems predominate and are of such general importance that they concern us all.

There is the problem of education. Shall the ideals of public education be subservient primarily to the past, the present, or the future? Shall the schools emphasize culture or vocation? These questions, burdened with consequences, are being decided in every community in conformity with one or other of the chief educational views which the last two decades have forced to the front; the view that the schools should somehow reinstate what is known as classical education because of its disciplinary and cultural effectiveness; the view that for practical reasons education should be modeled after business and factory with their ideals of efficiency, minimum overhead, large scale production, and uniformity of output; the view that public schools are the one means of steady social progress, and that consequently public education should aim to produce socially minded and socially effective human beings prepared to take a forward step in the realization of a more satisfactory communal life. Here is a chance for spiritual development. By intelligent, informed participation in the decision of this issue, by championing the interests of those who, though most concerned are naturally voiceless, the adult citizen broadens his interests, deepens his insight, and intensifies his concern for the higher life of his community.

A yet more intimate means to the same end is pride in good work. "I must tell you," writes a friend, "of M. Bachelin, the man who makes the most marvelous gateaux in Switzerland, and what he replied when I told him that in one year he could make his fortune in New York, and return to Switzerland with so much money that he would never have to work again: 'I thank you, monsieur, but I'm afraid I haven't your point of view. You don't understand; my aim is not to make money, but to make better and better cakes! I have enough money to live on; I never worry about that any more. I do, however, stay awake nights wondering what new idea I could think of in the way of cakes, and how I could make those I do make better and better and better. And I only hope that up to the day I die I shall still be able to think of new ideas for cakes, and new ways of making the old ones better. No, I suppose it's funny to an American, but I can't see where you have the advantage of us, with *all* your money. Undoubtedly your money makes you physically more comfortable, but does it make you happier?' "

Perhaps this observation presents a distorted view of the average American, though it may fairly represent the traveling specimens commonly met abroad. Still, no criticism is more common than that the laborer has lost or is losing all sense of workmanship, and there is little justification for limiting the criticism to any one class. The joy to be gained from doing good work for its own sake has come to have less and less of a place in the lives of men and women generally. In few people is it so utterly lacking that their work is in no wise affected by it; nevertheless for the vast majority it is a peripheral, not a central, interest. This unquestionably means a shrinking and degrading of personality. To remedy this defect is not a simple matter—except on paper. How shall joy in good work be associated with industry? with farming? with the hundred tedious occupations made inevitable by modern society? But whether simple or not, it is a great spiritual necessity. And something at least can be done by unnumbered individuals to win for themselves the personal quality which devotion to doing good work brings; something also to help institute conditions which shall provide a more favorable opportunity in this respect for others.

In a way analogous to this many inconspicuous people attain to a quiet resourcefulness and simple dignity, a warmth and beauty of inner life which makes them "the salt of the earth." According to the schools they are ignorant, but it is "a sweet and precious ignorance, the treasure of a pure soul at peace with itself." For they know the art of filling their places with skill and helpfulness and joy. Overlooked in chronicles of village or metropolis, rewarded by no medals, honored by no title, they do their work with cheerfulness and understanding, and radiate a perfume which sweetens all they touch. And when their dear forms have gone from us, the memory of the great souls they had become lingers as a solace and an incentive.

And no community is without its conflict between the tendency to ugliness and the tendency to beauty. Few cities or villages can claim to have withstood the commercial spirit in the interest of beauty of surroundings, if only for children and youth. "The purple patches of our great towns," as Galsworthy remarks, "are often as rouge on the cheeks and salve on the lips of a corpse." We support a group of artists, landscape gardeners, and the like, but they cannot protect us against, though they may blind us to, the ugliness which our esthetic indifference and our infatuation with material success constantly insinuate into life. The responsibility cannot be thus avoided. If the enjoyment of beauty is to be a common vital experience it must become a common vital interest. "Every time that any of us rearranges forms found in Nature," we were recently told, "into new presentations pleasing to himself he is an Artist. Every effort to present a harmonious as well as efficiently designed automobile or street lamp post is a sincere and important piece of art work. Every housewife who selects the fittings of her house with real concern that they shall suit and please her and who keeps the arrangement in accordance with the same personal standard is an Artist." All such efforts to add beauty to the everyday environment and to circumvent and defeat the encroachment of ugliness are episodes in the attainment of soul.

But there is no one way for all men to the acquisition of soul. Rather, there are as many ways as there are souls to be achieved. For some people it would mean to break through habitual frivolity and to catch a glimpse of the tragedy of human life; for others, to acquire a sense of humor, twin sister of tears. The way will not hide if the seeker be in earnest. Only let it be taken to heart that soul is not the name of a thing, but of a life; that the soul's salvation is not a commodity or gift to be bought or begged, but a development to be attained; that to save one's soul is not an instantaneous deed, but a lifelong adventure; not the rescue of an indefinable entity in preparation for a life to come, but the creation of a type of personality through loyalty to concrete values as these are at issue in everyday experience. It is an inner richness and ripeness, a sensitiveness to truth, to beauty, to the dignity of life.

CHAPTER XI

THE WAR AND THE GOD-MAKERS

IN a sense men have always made their gods. That fact was announced to the Greeks by Xenophanes in these words: "The Ethiopians make their gods black and snub-nosed; the Thracians say theirs have blue eyes and red hair. . . . Yes, and if oxen and horses or lions had hands, and could paint with their hands, and produce works of art as men do, horses would paint the forms of the gods like horses, and oxen like oxen, and make their bodies in the image of their several kinds." And A. E. Haydon puts it in this way: "The gods pass across the stage of history in forms innumerable: one note of pathos dominates the drama, man's longing for support, security, companionship, and help from the environing universe. The biography of every god is an epic into which are written the dreams and sorrows, tragedy and achievements of some human group. . . . The divine figures of our human story are therefore rooted in the social needs and aspirations of men. They grow and change with their people."

Men have always made their gods under stress of deeply felt need, but the creation was unconscious. The god was thought to be discovered, however much he was made. That is exactly the difference, we have been taught, between true believer and idolater, between Christian and heathen. The former worships the God that is, the latter bows down to his own creation. Atheists, agnostics, and the religiously indifferent have long been familiar in many varieties, nor is the world unacquainted with religious reformers, men who sought to clear away the theological or ceremonial underbrush which they believed choked up the approach to the temple of the living God. But the contemporary movement is something different. It is a self-conscious determination to dethrone the God of our fathers, and to replace him by a God elected on a platform of approved social and political ideals. As such it may be called a novel adventure in religion, and one which enables us to get a clearer view of the process.

The disfavor into which the God of our fathers has fallen was perhaps inevitable anyway (for humanity was on the point of outgrowing the ethics of its deity), but it was precipitated and intensified by the war. And for two reasons: because the war aroused the suspicion that in this great human crisis God was careful to maintain a strict neutrality; and because it forced upon men an appreciation of the problem of evil. From the point of view of logic, the war introduced no new element into the situation. Logically, one single small evil is as much a challenge to God's omnipotent goodness as a thousand large ones, and his accepted neutrality in the everyday crises of life is as serious as his aloofness when civilization itself seems to be at stake. As Chanticleer said: "An insect's death can teach us all disaster." This was long ago pointed out by John Stuart Mill, Frederic Harrison, William James, and others. Emotionally, however, the matter is quite different. A Lisbon earthquake, a Mont Pelée eruption, a war in which millions of human beings are slaughtered by other millions, these have power to break through the habitual somnolence of mortals, and to capture the imagination. Consequently the stupendous losses resulting from the war, its hideous brutalities and unbelievable hypocrisies, have forced many besides Mr. Britling to see it through. In the light of the world-conflagration men who had remained impervious to the logic of their position could no longer avoid seeing the crack in what was supposed to be somehow the perfect work of God.

Yet without another factor in the situation, even the war would have failed to produce this result.

The trouble is that theology has lost its grip upon life. Present day thinkers cannot avail themselves of concepts and beliefs which in the past were employed to rationalize and neutralize evil. However mystical we may be in other respects, we have become too naturalistic and too observant to accept the time-honored explanations. It is becoming increasingly difficult to persuade men that the ills and tragedies of life are either the unhappy consequences of the gift of free will to the first man, or the evidence of a just and righteous God's displeasure at sin, or the necessary means for the development of character.

The significance of this change is seen most clearly in the more spectacular aspect of our theological bankruptcy—the exile of His Satanic Majesty. When the air swarmed with evil spirits, and hell ran a double shift of imps, convulsions of nature or other catastrophes which brought ruin to human hopes appeared easy to explain without incriminating God. There was no reason why terrible scourges like the Black Death should shake the foundations of common belief. They were perfectly harmonious with the universe, and with life as then conceived; indeed, there was every reason why they should reënforce rather than undermine current views. Even in the more recent past, when the earthly representation of the nether region had been reduced to the omnipresent Tempter at every man's elbow, moral or physical disaster did not obviously do violence to God's omnipotence or perfect goodness.   There was still a being or principle of evil upon whom, or which, might be put the blame for every defect; a sort of cosmic goat, through whose sacrificial offices God was healed.   During the past generation, however, this Prince of Darkness has disappeared as a vital reality from the walks of men, together with all his crew and trappings. How necessary he was to the God with whom he had been so long associated is demonstrated by the present religious predicament.   With no devil to blame for a spiritual and material devastation too enormous to be blinked, attention is centered upon God as the responsible party.   "Do you mean to tell me," cries E. H. Reeman, "that there is a God who could end it all to-morrow if He wished, but that he won't?   I cannot believe it, and if I could I do not think I should have much use for such a God anyhow."   H. G. Wells is quite as direct and more biting.   "Why," he says in the person of his double, Mr. Britling, "if I thought there was an omnipotent God who looked down on battles and deaths and all the waste and horror of this war—able to prevent these things—doing them to amuse himself—I would spit in his empty face."

This reaction is not limited to laymen, although the fact that the literary output on the subject is so largely by laymen is an interesting aspect of the situation. The most burning challenge of all comes from Rev. G. A. Studdert Kennedy, a priest in the Church of England, who went out as a chaplain in 1915. The tenor of what this deeply religious man, trained in theology and acquainted with life, thought amid the hardship of the trenches and the brutalities of war may be gathered from this extract from his book, *The Hardest Part:*

"God is helpless to prevent war, or else He wills it and approves of it. There is the alternative. You pay your money and you take your choice. . . . If God wills war then I am morally mad and life has no meaning. I hate war, and if God wills it, I hate God, and I am a better man for hating Him; that is the pass it brings me to. In that case the first and great commandment is, 'Thou shalt hate the Lord thy God with all thy heart, and Him only shalt thou detest and despise.' "

These are typical. It is the same disjunctive that compels all to a new appreciation of the problem of evil: either we must have a new God, or make God responsible for the greatest moral catastrophe of history. Between two such alternatives no man,

they think, can hesitate to choose the former. All
of which is only another way of saying that in the
downfall of the orthodox God, the banished Satan
has his revenge.

Turning to the god-makers at work, the most
picturesque is easily Mr. Wells. No other breaks
into the sanctuaries with such will to destroy, or lays
about him there with such reckless energy. Nor
has he a rival as a builder and maker of new gods.
For Mr. Wells not only aims to rend the awful
Trinity into bits of theological fantasy, and to smash
the "bickering monopolist who will have none other
Gods but ME"; that "stuffed scare-crow of divinity" who is no better than "a Polynesian god of
sharks' teeth and painted wood and mother-of-
pearl"; he proposes to supply mankind with a new
Trinity and a new God.

There is first the Veiled Being, beyond all and
above all, "enigmatical and incomprehensible," which
"broods over the mirror upon which the busy shapes
of life are moving." The Veiled Being does not
concern itself about men, and men can have no
dealings with it. Then out of this inscrutable being
comes a lesser being, "as a wave comes rolling to
us from beyond the horizon." This is the Will to
Be, the Life Force, the Struggle for Existence. It
is a breeding, fighting thing. In it we live, as the

beasts live. Of it are our passions and desires and
fears. But neither of these is God. God is third
and least in the celestial triumvirate. "He is spirit,
. . . the immortal part and leader of mankind."
He is boundless, immortal youth, and thus naturally
boundless, immortal courage and boundless, immortal love. He is "our friend and brother and
the light of the world." After meeting him a man
"goes about the world like one who was lonely and
has found a lover, like one who was perplexed and
has found a solution." Some day he may even lead
the way to the Veiled Being!

Few if any of Mr. Wells' co-laborers would accept his pantheon or trade their God for his. Nor
would they trade among themselves. On one thing,
however, there is general agreement: the new God
must be finite; a God with no more than a fighting
chance. Here they leave no room for doubt. "The
fact that God is *finite*," writes Mr. Wells, "is one
upon which those who think clearly among the new
believers are very insistent." "God is neither all-
wise, nor all-powerful, nor omnipresent; . . . he
is neither the maker of heaven nor earth, and
. . . he has little to identify him with that hereditary God of the Jews who became the 'Father' in
the Christian system."

To such specific statements might be added scores

of passages which illustrate God's finiteness. For example, it is not at all certain, Mr. Wells reports, that God knows more about the ultimate nature and purpose of things than we do. "He hopes and attempts"—and, presumably, fails at times. Moreover, he needs our help to overcome his enemies. To this end "the true God goes through the world like fifes and drums and flags, calling for recruits along the street." Or, perhaps it were better to say he used to do so; for in a more recent account than *God the Invisible King*, he is relegated to a disorderly, cob-webbed office, leaving man to take hold of the world unassisted. But whether he is the "Great Adventurer" or the "Invisible King" or "a lean, tired, intelligent-looking oldish man, with an air of futile friendliness," or the "Undying Fire" (Mr. Wells has accumulated quite a museum of gods), he is at all events finite. Again and again the doctrine is reiterated, as if the writer were obsessed with the fear that some one might get away with a remnant of faith in a Lord God Almighty, maker of heaven and earth. Mr. Wells bears a strong family likeness to his own creation, Dodd, who constituted himself "a sort of alert customs officer to see that the Creator wasn't smuggled back" and who, according to Boon, every night "looked under his bed for the Deity, and slept with a large revolver under his pillow for fear of a revelation."

This determination to save the world by winning it from an omnipotent to a struggling God is raised to the rampant-militant degree by Studdert Kennedy, who in his message from the trenches declares: "It is the Almighty God we are fighting; He is the soul of Prussianism. I want to kill Him. That is what I'm here for. I want to kill the Almighty God and tear Him from His throne. It is Him we are really fighting against. I would gladly die to kill the idea of the Almighty God Who drives men either to cruelty or atheism."

The god offered to his fellow pilgrims by Mr. Reeman (an American god-maker) seems at first to fall below the required standard of incompetence. Mr. Reeman makes God "the indwelling life of the universe, of the remotest star and sun as well as our planet—the indwelling life of the clod as well as the soul." This God has produced the universe and all living forms. A tolerably respectable deity, one would say, or, at all events, much more of a deity than the Wellsian. Upon closer acquaintance, however, this first impression is not borne out. For it transpires that the indwelling, creating life-force of the infinite universe is after all very finite. We discover that the Life-Force-God began by making crude first experiments in self-expression, which resulted in the production of the inorganic world. Then came higher forms of self-expression. Sometimes it all had to be undone, of which the most striking example is the marvelous but tragic reptilian age. Finally, after unnumbered centuries, in a supreme effort, in a spurt of creative genius, as it were, God succeeded in producing man. But man is apparently the measure of his power. Nothing can be more obvious from the equally-balanced struggle between good and evil in the world, Mr. Reeman argues, than the fact that it has long been a case of nip and tuck between God's powers of coming to higher expression, and the thwarting forces arrayed against him. Even in so stupendous a contest between good and evil as the World War, where "His interests [were] as much at stake as humanity's," God was unable to accomplish enough to make it clear which side he was fighting on. In the face of hard facts, then, the only tenable view is that "God is actually now doing the best He can, and can't do better"; that he is in an extremity; that he needs assistance. It isn't homage or worship or prayers or hymns that he wants and needs, but "our brain, our blood, our will, our life." And if we refuse to come to his aid, it looks as if God might actually be defeated.

But the most graphic description of this finite God

is that of St. John Ervine in *Changing Winds*.
Speaking of the central character of the book at a
moment of great emotional crisis, he says, apparently in sympathy with the conception: "It seemed
to him that God was not a Being who miraculously
made the world, but a Being who labored at it, suffered and failed, and rose again and achieved. . . .
He could hear God, stumbling through the Universe, full of the agony of desire, calling continually, 'Let there be light!   Let there be light!' . . ."

The conception of God as finite is of course in no
sense a novelty.   To say nothing of the gods of
undeveloped peoples, which are invariably finite, nor
of the Greek and Roman gods, which were recognized to be in bondage to Fate, and not to enlarge
upon the fact that our own infinite God only grew to
his august proportions after centuries of development, the doctrine of the finiteness of God has been
defended specifically and repeatedly since Plato first
brought the idea into philosophy and gave it his
powerful backing.   Indeed, this very question
(whether the being called God is supreme in the
universe) appears to have been the source of much
of the bitter theological strife of the first centuries
of the Christian era.   Nor was it settled once for
all by the use of the steam-roller at the Council of
Nicæa.   Again and again in the course of the cen-

turies the ghost of the early controversy returned
to disturb the banquet spread by theological orthodoxy. The contemporary outbursts are in their better portions but faint echoes of discussions like that
of John Stuart Mill. It is all there in *Three Essays
on Religion*—except the rhapsody and the muddle.

In one respect, however, the contemporary movement is unique, namely, in the kind and degree of
finiteness demanded. It is not enough that God be
responsible to some more ultimate reality, as in the
case of Plato, to the Good; or that he be kept from
producing just the kind of world he would prefer,
by beings of a character far different from his own,
which was Mill's view. It is not even enough that
God be reduced to the extremity of requiring the
assistance of mankind to save him from defeat. He
must be a biased partisan in the social and political
struggles of the hour. They will have nothing to
do with "a God in an easy chair" (the phrase is
Mr. Reeman's); he must get into the game. "Hard
and practical men who want to get the world
straighter than it is," says Mr. Wells, "perceive that
they must have a leadership and reference outside
themselves"; and such leadership can only be found
in a God who takes a hand in affairs. Mr. Wells
put the situation concisely to Mr. David Lubin,
when they "lunched together in a pretty little room

high over Knightsbridge." "I told him," says Mr.
Wells, reporting the conversation for *The New Republic,* "that I had been coming more and more to
the idea—not as a sentimentality or a metaphor, but
as the ruling and directing idea, the structural idea,
of all one's political and social activities—of the
world as one state and community, and of God as
King of that state."

Very good. But in what visible form is this invisible King of the World to redeem himself from
metaphor? On that important question Mr. Wells
remains tantalizingly vague. Nor does the Rev.
Mr. Kennedy make clear the earthly incarnation of
the finite God, unless, perhaps, in these words at
the conclusion of his chapter entitled, "God and
Democracy": "If any king survives it will be ours,
for he is very nearly a 'Christian King.' The crown
of our British Kings is a crown of golden thorns."

In spite of vagueness and ambiguity, it is perhaps
not impossible to determine what these gentlemen
intend. Once again, however, it is Mr. Reeman
who promulgates the idea with commendable direct-
ness. The mystic power at the heart of the universe must be reinterpreted "in the terms of modern
democratic outreach." The world-wide social movement of which we are witness is ultimately as much
a negation of monarchy and oligarchy in religion as

in politics. "When the crown falls and the throne crumbles in social government, then, indeed," according to Mr. Reeman, "it follows Vox Populi, Vox Dei. Democracy takes the scepter of kingliness out of the hand of the monarch, and places it in the hand of the hewer of wood and drawer of water, in order to show that he, too, is of the same stuff of which kings are made." Nor can God any longer escape this leveling process. "When a nation that has repudiated monarchy in government takes time to reflect," says Mr. Reeman, "it will surely not be long before it sees the practical impossibility of retaining in theology what it has felt bound to reject in politics." It is inevitable therefore that America, historically the foremost exponent of the democratic "urge" and "outreach" of the universe, and only yesterday the leader in making the world safe for democracy, shall presently engage in the larger task of making God safe for democracy. This is the heart of the new theology. We must have a new God, for both theoretical and practical reasons, a God of the people, by the people, and for the people.

Now what may be expected to result from the labors of the contemporary god-makers and the forces which have set them to work? The full answer is of course in the keeping of sure-handed time, but a guess or two may be ventured. And, first of all, there is little reason to doubt that the vast majority of religious people will reject this finite God. For the mass of believers God is compensatory, whatever else he may be; he makes good the defects and defeats of mortal existence. He transforms the evil that would otherwise be unbearable into an illusion or a good in disguise; he stands with the embattled idealist, and makes him the unconquerable majority; he enables man to triumph over the unavoidable defeat called death. No single definition of religion can do justice to the great variety of moods and creeds and activities which the term religion has covered in the course of time and covers to-day, but it is much more nearly right than wrong to say that religion is an adventure in comradeship with what is regarded as enduring within or underneath the drift and waste of time. Whatever peculiarities of creed or ceremony or practice religion may here or there take on, the essence of it is expressed in the well-known hymn, which for that very reason, retains a perennial freshness:

Swift to its close ebbs out life's little day;
Earth's joys grow dim, its glories pass away;
Change and decay in all around I see;
O thou, who changest not, abide with me!

This refusal to be psychically alone in a material universe, as John Fiske would have put it, this impulse to view the temporal under the form of eternity, as Spinoza would have said, this craving for a "Father of lights, with whom is no variableness, neither shadow of turning," as we may express it for the plain man, will recognize no resemblance to God in a being who is "most imperfect, often erring, like any one of us"; to say nothing of a being stumbling through the universe, calling in blindness and agony for light. To the vast majority who worship a God at all, he will be what he was to Isaiah—he "who hath measured the waters in the hollow of his hand, and meted out heaven with the span," to whom "the nations are as a drop of a bucket," and "who taketh up the isles as a very little thing." They will worship a pure abstraction, provided it may be called infinite, but not a finite being, though he be credited with interest in the latest fashions in ideals. They will find nothing appealing in a movement which is headed in the direction of making God a cosmic bell-boy.

There are, however, people of another temper, people who are far less interested in the nature and attributes of God than in having intimacies with him or in being assured of his partiality to mankind. They will not shrink from dwarfing God to human standards, since their whole working philosophy is based upon the naïve assumption that whatever is valued by man must be of vital concern to God. And they are not without the support of tradition. From the beginning of theological speculation those who emphasized the scripture, "For as the heavens are higher than the earth, so are my ways higher than your ways, and my thoughts than your thoughts," have been opposed by others who stressed passages referring to one who "was in all points tempted like as we are, yet without sin"; those who were ever in search of a concept of God that might more nearly do justice to his infinite remove from finite human nature, have been opposed by others who employed every logical and literary ingenuity to bridge the gap between the two. And this tendency to humanize God has received new impetus from every advance of humanism.

There are men and women, then, who will gladly respond to appeals like those we have considered. To them the hope of an alliance with "a God fighting out His battles and needing all the help that we can give to win the victory" will supply a new incentive to noble effort, by giving new dignity and horizon to conduct. They will not be repulsed but rather attracted by the gallantry and dash of the writers, and the reported geniality, good nature, and heroism of the finite God. They will not object to a come-on-fellows-what-do-you-care sort of re-

ligion, and a strapping big brother sort of divinity.
It is no accident that Studdert Kennedy's book bears
the imprint of the Y.M.C.A., and was issued by that
organization for the American Expeditionary Forces
in France. Besides, many people who might ordinarily be antagonistic to this conception of religion
and of deity, yet feel so deep a need of an anthro-
pomorphic God, and are so completely out of touch
with the conceptions presented in our sermons and
hymns, that they are prepared to find something
vital in any new conception without examining nar-
rowly into its logical or moral credentials.

A third class, not so large as either of the fore-
going, but in the end of great importance, will find
it difficult to take these writers seriously. Readers
accustomed to even moderate rigor of thought will
be repelled by the logical nonchalance of the new
theologians and will be surprised at their seeming
innocence of the literature of the subject. Earnest,
sincere, public-spirited men the writers obviously
are; but it is quite as obvious that they show a merry
disregard for exact thinking and a happy-go-lucky
indifference to the complexities of the problem which
others have found it difficult to wrestle with. In
the presence of evil (which we are led to think is
now appreciated for the first time) there are but
two alternatives, we are told. Either God is all-

good but not all-powerful, or all-powerful but not all-good. Well, other alternatives have been suggested, and one wonders why they are here ignored. There is the alternative offered by John Fiske on behalf of Cosmic Theism, and the alternative of Josiah Royce, the philosophic idealist—to mention no others. (Royce used to say that such treatments of the subject as we have been considering made him think of little children playing bare foot in the shallow edges of the sea.) Fiske's view that God is both all-powerful and all-good, but that evil (as we regard it) performs a necessary function in the gradual upward evolution of life, or Royce's view that evil is essential to the perfection of the Absolute, may not be satisfactory views to the Rev. Mr. Kennedy, Mr. Reeman, and Mr. Wells, but they are not justified in ignoring them.

Finally, it will probably turn out that the protagonists of the new gods overshot their mark, so that instead of introducing men to "a new and more vital faith in God" as they earnestly hoped, they helped men to do without such faith altogether. There are two reasons for anticipating this result. Once convince a man that logically only a God who is finite, that is to say more or less incompetent, can be interested in human beings and their projects, and one of two things is likely to happen. Either he will return to the view that God is infinite, and that therefore all thought of coöperative relationship between him and man is pure romanticism; or he will accept the alternative that God is finite, and sooner or later come to believe that he is negligible. In either case God ceases to be a vital reality. The conflict is well put by Gratian in Galsworthy's *Saint's Progress*. Gratian is talking with her father, a parson, while her husband of six months is lying in a stupor, hovering between life and death:

"There is no God, Dad."

"My darling child, what are you saying?"

"No God who can *help* us; I feel it. If there were any God who can take part in our lives, alter anything without our will, knew or cared what we did—He wouldn't let the world go on as it does."

"But, my dear, His purposes are inscrutable. We dare not say He should not do this or that, or try to fathom to what ends He is working."

"Then He's no good to us. It's the same as if He didn't exist. Why should I pray for George's life to One whose ends are just His own? I *know* George oughtn't to die. If there's a God who can help, it's a wicked shame when babies die, and all these millions of poor boys. I would rather think there's no God than a helpless or a wicked God—"

.   .   .   .

"My darling, you're overtired."

"No, Dad." She raised her head from his shoulder and, clasping her hands round her knees, looked straight before her. "We can only help ourselves; and I can only bear it if I rebel."

The fact that an infinite God is necessarily aloof from human affairs, unmoved alike by our joys and our tears, has been so often contended for by thinkers of the first order that the position is not a novelty. And if it has not been customary in the same manner to develop the doctrine of the finite God to its logical conclusion—as it has not—this has been due to a curious fact, namely, that the argument for God's finiteness has always included a proviso. God was held to be finite in knowledge and power, but infinite in goodness. It is precisely this perfection of character which, as we have seen, motivates the whole propaganda for a finite God. But if we insist that God may make mistakes and be defeated, like any one of us, what logical ground is there for maintaining that he can do no wrong? There would seem to be none. If similar to a human being in one respect, why not in another? The men we have been considering, as well as Mill, Harrison, James, and others who have felt compelled by a sense of the reality of evil to insist upon the finiteness of God, have always at the same time insisted upon or tacitly assumed his ideal goodness. It is not at all impossible, however, that their disciples, living in an era of extraordinary self-assertion, may take the next step. Having been persuaded that God is not as wise or as powerful as he might be, they may become bold enough to add that he isn't as good as he might be either. If the masters can retain their rationality only by concluding that God is doing the best he can with the limited wisdom and power at his disposal—and this they insist upon—the disciples may find it necessary, for the same reason, to conclude that God is as good as he can be in view of his moral limitations. And what if they then refrain (in May Sinclair's phrase) from "whitewashing God"? Having proceeded in emancipation so far, what is to hinder them from going further and urging their fellows, with all the earnestness and zeal for social regeneration characteristic of their masters, to try the hypothesis that there is no supernatural being of any sort that cares to, or can, assist men in the furtherance of human desires? Certain thinkers, to be sure, favor trying out this hypothesis, as various God-hypotheses have been tried out, and predict that happy results would follow the experiment. Obviously, however, the champions of the finite God are not in this class. They are quite as convinced as those who believe in the infinite God, that the attempt to operate without some sort of faith in a divinity that shapes our ends, can lead only to disaster. Nevertheless the very arguments they use to prove that God is finite will go a long way towards proving either that his existence is doubtful, or that he may be left out of account. They come as voices in the wilderness, heralding a new God; it may be their fate to be received as pioneers of a new agnosticism.

But whatever may be the final outcome of the contemporary movement to re-fashion God, one good result is already apparent—attention is being fastened upon the function of the God-idea in human existence. It is no longer above challenge. After all, the movement is only the logical development of the assertion of Jesus that the sabbath was made for man, not man for the sabbath. May Sinclair, on behalf of absolutism, has great fun playing philosophical rough-house with this temper in religion, and Paul Elmer More, on behalf of classicism, finds ever new occasion to ridicule the spirit that questions any of the "eternal verities." They will have their followers. So will the new god-makers, in so far as they are more determined to prove all things than fearful lest they fail to hold fast that which is good. Whether they lead men away from, or to a new faith in supernatural beings, remains to be seen, but the world-wide religious and ethical unrest of which they are symptomatic can scarcely fail to deepen and enrich life since it encourages examination into the bearing of faith in God on man's earthly concerns. It draws attention very sharply to the compensatory function which religion performs and to the reason why the gods have risen and fallen. Meanwhile one wonders, in these days of the church's material expansion, how accurately Wells has described the leaders of the churches in this crisis: "Men intelligent and enquiring and religiously disposed, all lying like overladen camels . . . outside the needle's eye that leads to God."

CHAPTER XII

THE HUNGER FOR COSMIC SUPPORT

For days and days together growing crowds of men and women tramped over hot, dusty roads, headed for a little gem of blue water set in a circle of many-colored hills in northern Palestine. The report had spread abroad that a young man was passing through the coast towns of the Sea of Galilee, teaching about ultimate matters with unheard-of freshness. He was said to bring hope to the discouraged, health to the sick, uneasiness to the mighty. It was this young man they sought. And when they found him—perhaps on a hillside with a crowd gathered at his feet, or teaching from a boat at the edge of the sea to the multitude that would otherwise press too close; sometimes early in the morning in a secluded place of prayer, or again in the cool of evening, at his temporary abode, surrounded by those brought to him suffering from all manner of diseases—wherever it was, when they found him they surrendered one by one to his unique personality. There was something so engaging yet noble

in his bearing, something so simple yet profound in
his thought, something so poetic yet vital in his
speech, something so sad yet healing in his smile
that, presently, turning to one another, they whis-
pered, "Never man spake like this man."

Which is by no means to say that they understood
him. They were won by his personal charm and
impressed by his exhibition of power, but they misunderstood his message and failed to catch his spirit.
He announced a new era based upon the principle
of human equality; they forthwith fell to wondering and then to disputing which of them should have
the chief advantage from the revolution. He urged
a change of heart as the first essential to the changed
order; their minds perpetually revolved about a re-
arrangement of possessions. So it happened that
one of his most impressive discourses was devoted
to this issue. On a certain occasion when the throng
pressed about him and when even those nearest to
his thought, the men he had chosen to carry his
message to the world, were in a wrangle as to the
exact dignity each was to possess in the coming kingdom, he spoke his mind on the subject. From that
discourse a searching question has come down to us.
It is recorded in three of the four biographical
sketches we have of his life, and, as we have been
taught, it runs thus:

What shall it profit a man, if he shall gain the whole world, and lose his own soul?

Three years after coming to public notice (or perhaps it was only one year, as some think) the young leader was dead. Persons of influence had secured his arrest, and had aroused the populace against him. He got the sort of trial a social pioneer usually gets, was sentenced to death by a judge who confessed he could discover no guilt in him, was led out to the hill of execution, a curious throng crowding in train. His friends deserted him or were awed into silence. The more brutal or ignorant of the rabble jeered and mocked. There, on the central cross of three, black against the evening sky, his great spirit took flight. The crowd strolled back, gossiping, joking, jostling one another through the city gate. Night settled down, the stars came out, Jerusalem slept. And the young Galilean slept soundest of all. So quickly may even a significant life be snuffed out. Or seem to be snuffed out. For it is now clear enough that the challenge of that brief life has come down the centuries. We still ask, and with new insistence:

What shall it profit a man, if he shall gain the whole world, and lose his own soul?

For all that, the meaning of the question is far from obvious. Doubtless it is a question in form only, the thought being categorical. We are meant to understand that no matter what a man accumulates, no matter what he gathers together, if in this gaining he loses his soul, the loss is greater than the gain and the sum is failure; in a word, that the man who loses his soul is bankrupt. This much is clear. Beyond this, however, the citation bristles with questions. What is meant by the "world" in the gaining of which one runs such risks? What is meant by the "soul" which is so highly valued? What does it mean to "lose" this so highly valued soul? Furthermore, are the alternatives—world and soul—mutually exclusive? Are the goods of life and the life of the soul absolutely incompatible, so that to the extent one is gained the other is lost? Or is there a point beyond which any further gaining of the world involves a corresponding loss of soul?

The early church answered all these questions in clean-cut fashion, and in doing so gave a turn to the conception of the higher life under which we still operate. The world was the complexity of people, institutions, goods, enjoyments, activities with which men commonly busy themselves. The soul was a spiritual entity temporarily imprisoned

in a corrupt and corruptible body, but destined to
be freed in due time to live in a heaven of unutter-
able bliss or a hell of unspeakable torment forever.
To lose this soul was to seek satisfaction in the
world and in consequence to fail of the inner regeneration upon which eternal felicity depended.
Nor did a compromise way of life appear possible.
The revolutionary feature of Christian philosophy
was exactly its insistence upon the renunciation of
the goods men naturally aim to secure and the obligations men naturally acknowledge.   For allegiance to these things that are seen but pass away
was substituted allegiance to the things that are not
seen but abide, while the everyday social and civic
loyalties were replaced by a desire to do the will
of the supernatural Ruler of the universe.   This is
why we say that Christianity revalued all values.
Life got a new polarity.   It became the rehearsal
for a transcendental drama to be staged in the "city
which hath foundations, whose builder and maker is
God."   In and of itself, life on earth had neither
worth nor significance.

Is this what the Man of Galilee intended?   It
would seem not.   If one reads the Markian or earliest account of the movement which made its appeal
to men under the slogan, "The Good News," and
reads it as one does the report of other social phe-

nomena, one gets an unmistakable sense of the importance of the here and now.   The whole story has the healthy smell of earth upon it.   Disdain of human beings with their everyday ties and occupations is certainly not the dominant tone of the narrative, if it is present at all.   Indeed the common business of living, permeated by a new spirit, is exalted and glorified.

The burden of the discourses is the urgent need for a manner of life free from economic injustice and religious formalism.   It is true that the new order is referred to as the kingdom of God, but this need only mean that the change was to be thoroughgoing, a change in the very spirit, not merely the outward form of life, and that such change was thought to bring the earthly economy into accord with the spiritual reality at the heart of things.   Life was to be shifted from a possessive to a non-possessive basis, and religion from conventional observance of rites to vital participation in the good life.   Men were to become brothers in the adventure of improving their common earthly lot, and this spirit of brotherhood once attained, all things needful should be added unto them.   If it is only by a strained interpretation that some recent writers have been able to make it appear that the origin of Christianity was a proletarian uprising led by a carpenter from Nazareth, it is by an interpretation no less strained that the learned doctors have been able to make it appear that the whole story is of other-worldly import. Whatever else the record discloses it is clear that the young Nazarene who taught for a brief but glorious season in Palestine regarded it as his mission to arouse mankind to the possibility of a more abundant life on earth.

How did it happen then that Christianity early received the supernatural intent which it retained through the centuries? The full explanation is a long story, but roughly speaking two factors may be singled out as mainly responsible: one, the public execution of the Galilean idealist at the beginning of his career; the other, the rise of a new leader, a remarkable youth from the city of Tarsus. On the highway to Damascus he was suddenly overwhelmed by a shining apparition of the recently crucified Jesus, and thereupon dedicated his life to the movement he had hitherto despised. It was Paul who rallied the adherents of what threatened to become a lost cause. And he was able to do this by inspiring them with a profoundly new conception of their revolutionary project. Paul came to his task with a very different cultural background from that of Jesus. He had been deeply influenced by the Greek-Oriental mystical tradition, and this influence injected itself into his conception of the movement he espoused. In this new conception the crucifixion was not, as it must have seemed to most, the unhappy end of a thwarted or misguided idealism, but the divinely ordained climax in the life and work of the long awaited Messiah. And the Messiah was no longer regarded as mortal, but the divine Logus or Reason manifested in the flesh. In Paul's teaching, therefore, the cross on Golgotha was transformed from a sign of defeat into a symbol of victory. It was the central fact in God's plan for the salvage of man's spiritual heritage, and, incidentally, the most important event of human history.

It was Paul the first organizer, theologian, philosopher of the Christian movement, a genius at propaganda, a man of versatile mind and tireless spirit, who gave Christianity its distinctly other-worldly emphasis. In contrast with his master's outdoor discourses on the art of living, Paul's writings are learned theological disquisitions on the purposes of God and the technicalities of salvation. In his view the chief problem of man is not how to improve his lot on earth through the establishment of a juster social economy, but how to win life everlasting in the world to come through faith in the divine plan of redemption. Conditions were ripe for a philosophy of world denial. For two centuries and more the drift had been steadily in that direction. The zealous leadership of Paul gave a new momentum to this drift, and Paulinian theology provided a comprehensive rationalization of the widespread and deep-going loss of moral nerve characteristic of the period. The belief grew that the existing order was on the verge of collapse, to be replaced by a commonwealth of the redeemed under the regency of the returned Son of God. Consequently man as man became base, life on earth vain and profitless, the one thing worth striving for the crown of approval which "the Lord, the righteous judge," would give to all them that loved his appearing.

This transformation of a social idealism into a supernatural cult is a striking instance of what has occurred again and again in human history. Since man became aware of himself as in a world other than himself, every attempt to deal in a straightforward manner with the world, to look it directly in the face and to adjust life to this view, has been opposed and circumvented by a counter attempt to give facts and events a supernatural interpretation. Nothing has been more powerful than the tendency to regard the sensible world as "a disheartening whirlwind of vain and fragmentary facts," utterly without meaning unless converted, through the laborious use of reason, into a hieroglyphic of divine purpose or an apparition of God. Scarcely had the scientific school of Miletus, which set out to leave off telling tales about the world and instead to study and describe it, culminated in the scientific naturalism of Democritus when it was overwhelmed by a wave of transcendentalism from Athens, to be followed in time by wave upon wave of Christian theology. In a like manner when, after an almost interminable night, day once more dawned; when through the voyages of the great navigators and the discovery of the telescope and microscope, men were introduced to a new earth, a new heavens, and a new world of microscopic life—all this new knowledge was feverishly exploited in the interest of supernaturalism. Natural theologies, as they were called, often beautifully bound and richly illustrated, issued in unbelievable numbers from the press, intent upon giving a supernatural coloring to this wealth of new data. The same thing happened again in the case of evolution. Even while the battle was still on over the naturalistic origin of man, Darwinism was given a supernaturalistic twist. Men were told that to look upon evolution naturalistically was to see it out of focus. They must see it as a supernatural scheme to bring mankind to perfection in order to get its true proportions. Said John Fiske:

"With Darwin's biology we rise to a higher view of the workings of God and the nature of man than was ever attainable before. So far from degrading humanity, or putting it on a par with the animal world in general, the Darwinian theory shows us definitely, and for the first time, how the creation and the perfection of man is the goal towards which Nature's work has all the while been tending."

And in the immediate present, enormously rich in scientific achievements and projects for the future, we witness the unusual phenomenon of an outspoken alliance, offensive and defensive, between the laboratory and the church, against all who would take their naturalism straight.

Inadequate as any such meager summary must be, it yet suggests how insistent and powerful has been and still is man's determination to view the drama of life from the wings of the cosmic stage, a determination the more singular since each new report of the vision to be gained from this vantage point has made delusions of the rest, only to be itself in like manner reduced to vanity. So ontologies and theodicies have steadily vanished under the weight of their successors, as the surface of the earth has repeatedly been buried under later deposits. Great thinkers have deployed an interesting array of facts, have won the devotion of disciples, but after centuries of searching man must still confess:

"Into this Universe, and *Why* not knowing
Nor *Whence*, like Water willy-nilly flowing;
And out of it, as Wind along the Waste,
I know not *Whither*, willy-nilly blowing."

Why is the venture not given up?   Across innumerable attempts is written at last:

"There was the Door to which I found no Key;
There was the Veil through which I might not see."

Why, then, do ever new searchers take up the task?
Rebuffed, defeated, what is it that urges them on?

It is the same thing which was felt by our brothers
and sisters who have slept through millenniums in
the sands of the East and which will stir to like
activity men and women to whom our times will
be as the times of Tut-Ankh-Amen are to us.   For
there is a rock fact of human nature against which
the waves of rhetoric and logic dash in vain; a rock
fact which, after all the proofs and disproofs have
fallen back into the sea of words from which they
came, stands forth the clearer for the spray dashed
over it.   What is this stubborn fact?   It is the fact
that human beings refuse to be psychically alone in
the universe; the fact that they demand that somehow there shall be a Power at the heart of things

which will not let them suffer ultimate defeat, let appearances be what they may.

Cosmologies become obsolete and creeds change; it is the fate of the intellectual symbols eventually to be looked upon as primitive and childish. But men in general feel with Fiske, that however cumbrous and obsolete these formulations may be in detail (as the necessity once so keenly felt by our forefathers, that man must occupy the largest and most central spot in the universe), they rest upon a fundamental truth which mankind can never safely lose sight of, namely, that human affairs are the chief object of God's care. "Once dethrone humanity," he argued, "regard it as a mere local incident in an endless and aimless series of cosmical changes, and you arrive at a doctrine which, under whatever specious name it may be veiled, is at bottom nothing more nor less than Atheism." Then all purpose vanishes from the cosmos. The universe becomes a box of toys or a house of cards, and all meaning vanishes from human life.

In the same vein one of the foremost scientists of our time writes: "If there be a man who does not believe, either through the promptings of his religious faith or through the objective evidence which the evolutionary history of the world offers, in a progressive revelation of God to man, if there be a man who in neither of these two ways has come to feel that there is a meaning to and a purpose for existence, if there be such thoroughgoing pessimism in this world, then may I and mine be kept as far as possible from contact with it. If the beauty, the meaning and the purpose of this life as revealed by both science and religion are all a dream, then let me dream on forever."

Let me dream on forever! In this cry we get a clew to the nature of the demand for cosmic support. It is emotional, not intellectual. Though we may be told that nothing short of the assumption of a purposive universe, in which man's higher development is definitely aimed at, can save us from *intellectual* confusion, it is not the fear of this, but of *emotional* confusion which gives the demand its vitality. If in the face of consistent intellectual defeat the result is not resignation but change of front, may we not conclude that the search for cosmic purpose, for the everlasting arms underneath, for psychic kinship with what Edwyn Bevan has called, "a Friend behind phenomena," has its source in the non-intellectual side of man's nature?

And if we do not oversimplify too much we must agree that men do not live by logic alone. No human being would be completely described were we able to catalogue his sense experiences, his thoughts, his memories, his castles in air. For sensations, thought, memories, imaginings, are saturated with feeling as all things in physical nature are said to be saturated with ether. Sometimes the emotional element is present like the gentle swell on the bosom of a quiet sea, at other times it rolls and tosses like irresistible breakers, washing away what labor and pains had slowly erected, leaving ruin and regret, or relief and joy in the wake of the storm. But always it is present, oozing into every crevice, searching out all interstices, inundating the remotest bounds of personality. The logically best society may turn up its nose at the tang and piquancy of emotion; may attempt to set up an exclusive intellectual quarter out of its reach, where no weeds of fallacy or wild flowers of fancy shall be permitted to grow, where syllogistic order and calm shall reign unchallenged. Life will overflow any such endeavor and be the richer for it.

But to recognize the inevitability and worth of feeling is not to admit that everything that is longed for is actually there to be had. And the fact that man naturally objects to being quite alone in the universe, and thus craves fellowship with a great Guarantor of his interests and his personal continuance, is no proof that anything corresponding to the object of this longing exists. It may rather testify to the vestigial remains of an elemental hunger brought down from the dim past, and transfigured by all manner of accretions through institutions and customs. Gilbert Murray has this interesting hint in his admirable study of the Stoics:

"We are gregarious animals; our ancestors have been such for countless ages. We cannot help looking out on the world as gregarious animals do; we see it in terms of humanity and of fellowship. Students of animals under domestication have shown us how the habits of a gregarious creature, taken away from his kind, are shaped in a thousand details by reference to the lost pack which is no longer there —the pack which a dog tries to smell his way back to all the time he is out walking, the pack he calls to for help when danger threatens. It is a strange and touching thing, this eternal hunger of the gregarious animal for the herd of friends who are not there. And it may be, it may very possibly be, that, in the matter of this Friend behind phenomena, our own yearning and our almost ineradicable instinctive conviction, since they are certainly not founded on either reason or observation, are in origin the groping of a lonely-souled gregarious animal to find its herd or its herd leader in the great spaces between the stars."

Much might be gained by acting on this hint. What noble things might be accomplished if we recognized in our insistence upon cosmic companionship a deflection of the desire for fellowship with our kind, and in the craving for transcendental support of our ideals a distortion of our deep interest in human well-being and progress! For John Dewey is right: "God only knows how many of the sufferings of life are due to a belief that the natural scene and operations of our life are lacking in ideal import, and to the consequent tendency to flee for the lacking ideal factors to some other world inhabited exclusively by ideals."

One tragic result of our diverted aspiration is that the conditions of life are fixed by those who have no concern for human destiny, either in this world or any other. There have always been men who, granted earthly success, were willing, like Macbeth, "to jump the life to come." That they have urged the mass of mankind to be faithful to their orisons, have indeed insisted upon this, is true enough. They have often been superstitious, even if not idealistic, and they have sometimes been unscrupulously clever, persuading us to fasten our eyes upon the sky that they might the more readily relieve us of things which we are slow to surrender voluntarily and deliberately. In any case, while unbelievable control has been won over natural forces, opening up almost unlimited opportunities for improving the conditions of life, it is a fact almost too notorious to bear mentioning again that the right to exploit these resources has passed into the hands of those who have been able to seize them and to turn them to their own advantage. It has always been a step towards a more worthy social economy, towards a better general chance at a more fortunate existence, when men and women have refused to be put off with the promise of a supernatural recompense for actual earthly defeat; when they have dared to entrust their destiny to the social devices their combined aspiration and intelligence might invent.

It is thus a constructive social suggestion that we endeavor to give up, as the basis of our desire to win a satisfactory life, the quest for the companionship with a being behind or within the fleeting aspect of nature; that we assume the universe to be indifferent towards the human venture that means everything to us; that we acknowledge ourselves to be adrift in infinite space on our little earth, the sole custodians of our ideals. There need be no spirit of defiance in this, no bitterness, no shrill declaration that

"It matters not how strait the gate,
How charged with punishments the scroll,

I am the master of my fate:
I am the captain of my soul."

Defiance testifies that the challenge has not really been accepted. No; accept the stern condition of being psychically alone in all the reach of space and time, that we may then, with new zest, enter the warm valley of earthly existence—warm with human impulse, aspiration, and affection, warm with the unconquerable thing called life; turn from the recognition of our cosmic isolation to a new sense of human togetherness, and so discover in a growing human solidarity, in a progressively ennobled humanity, in an increasing joy in living, the goal we have all along blindly sought, and build on earth the fair city we have looked for in a compensatory world beyond.

This is the challenge of these supreme times. The hope of a new world is alive to-day in millions of hearts the world around. May we not take courage from past achievement? No single one of us has passively accepted life; we have all insisted upon remaking it. Looked at from day to day little may seem to be accomplished, and yet what a series of victories a human being wins in a lifetime! Unconsciously, at first, and then more and more consciously, we have refused to feel at home in the world as we found it, but have insisted upon finding a world in which we could feel at home. Disillusions have not permanently disheartened us; defeats have balked us only for a time; in the very ruins of our hope we have found material for new dreams. In spite of squalor and meanness and vice there are few men of whom this may not be said in some degree. Even at the bier of one who has been stranger to great aspiration (type of the inglorious mass of us), we may, much more often than not, say in Stevenson's words: "Give him a march with his old bones; there, out of the glorious sun-colored earth, out of the day and the dust and the ecstasy —there goes another Faithful Failure!"

And the record of the individual is magnified in the achievement of the race. Laboriously the progenitor of man separated himself off from the brutes. With indescribable slowness the scope of life was enlarged, its rude economy enriched by discovery and invention, and beautified by the rise and development of the arts. Gradually the periphery of interest in others was pushed out, so that whereas it was once inconceivable for a man to be vitally concerned for the welfare of any one beyond the confines of his tribe, the time came when Terence could say, "I deem nothing alien to my feelings that concerns a human being." Granted that this outlook has never become the universal point of view, and that periodically great sections of mankind have been swept back into an attitude more nearly resembling the spirit of the tribe, yet in spite of stumblings and oscillations great progress has been made in the development of an intergroup, an international, and an interracial imagination, and much has been done in the way of creating instruments to make this imagination practically effective.

While it is true that tribal feelings can be aroused, the appeal which arouses them must now be made on a plane quite foreign to the tribal mind. Pure tribal spirit has been outgrown, and the trend of human emotions is away from it; so distinctly away from it that the outstanding temper of our day may be said to be the audacious hope of re-creating the world in the interest of all mankind. The hope may indeed come to little, for there are numerous obstacles in the way of its realization, but the hope itself is a great achievement, testifying to the momentum of the forces that actualize themselves in human life as social idealism. All this may encourage us to believe that a new world is possible—if we will.

To save human life from ultimate defeat may indeed be out of the question, for the cosmos appears indifferent to the drama enacted on our planet.

But, after all, nothing can defeat man but man himself. It is predicted that as the earth now sleeps every year for a winter, as we sleep every day for a night, so by and by the earth shall refuse to awake, as we rest at last in the sleep that nothing disturbs. It is predicted that then the uninhabited earth shall, like the moon, "roll its pale corpse in space," until it collides with the no-longer procreant sun, and the whole lifeless mass, ignited by the terrific shock, shall burst, to float a gigantic fiery veil in the boundless vast.

Let it be so. Meanwhile millions upon millions of human beings will strive and suffer and enjoy. They will suffer more and more and enjoy less and less, or suffer less and less and enjoy more and more. And the chief source of their misery or happiness will be human beings and the structure of society. It will be defeat if in the distant future the coöperative adventure of making human life richer and happier is interrupted by a change in the cosmic weather, but a kind of defeat which is at the same time the highest form of victory. *Real* defeat will overtake humanity only in so far as men themselves, forgetting that they are comrades in doom and agents of each other's woe or weal, go down the years estranged from the one friend they have— each other.

NOTES

These notes are not intended primarily to substantiate statements made or to facilitate the exact location of quotations, but to aid those who wish to go a little more fully into the subjects considered.

Numbers at the beginning of paragraphs refer back to pages on which the quotation or topic occurs.*

CHAPTER I

Hast Any Philosophy in Thee, Shepherd?

(3)* G. K. Chesterton's remark about the importance of philosophy appeared in *Heretics* (JOHN LANE COMPANY, 1906), as follows:

> But there are some people, nevertheless—and I am one of them—who think that the most practical and important thing about a man is still his view of the universe. We think that for a landlady considering a lodger, it is important to know his income, but still more important to know his philosophy. We think that for a general about to fight an enemy, it is important to know the enemy's numbers, but still more important to know the enemy's philosophy. We think the question is not whether the theory of the cosmos affects matters, but whether, in the long run, anything else affects them. (pp. 15-16)

The passage sounds convincing? Would it sound convincing if the meaning of philosophy did not vacillate?

(3) William James's comment on the passage is found in his *Pragmatism* (LONGMANS, GREEN & Co., 1907), p. 3. John Dewey approved of the doctrine in passing.

An item of interest in this connection recently appeared in *The New Republic* (Vol. XXXVII, p. 296). Edwin E. Slosson, Director of Science Service, has been making a collection of the notions which the average layman has of the world about him. The following are some of the more prevalent ones:

People are descended from "monkeys"; the sun is made of radium; Mars is inhabited by a race of canal diggers; the ancient Mayas knew all about relativity; the earth is getting hotter; the earth is getting colder; the earth will be smashed up by running into a comet; the average mental age of Americans is thirteen; all progress comes from a superior Nordic race; mankind is losing all its teeth and hair; the world is going to starve to death from over-population; the world is going to die off from race suicide; Conan Doyle proved the existence of fairies; drinking sour milk or grafting goat glands will make everybody live to 150; there is no soul; everybody has two or three souls; according to Freud you must give rein to every impulse or die of a complex; all rheumatism comes from bad teeth; all diseases can be cured by manipulating the back-bone; harnessing the power of the tides will replace coal as a source of power.

(4) The quotation from G. R. Dodson is from *Bergson and the Modern Spirit* (AMERICAN UNITARIAN ASSOCIATION, 1913), pp. 10-11. During the last few years this fact (that our former philosophical and theological creeds have lost their power) has been emphasized again and again.

The view that philosophy concerns itself with the whole of things is well stated in J. E. Leighton's *Man and the Cosmos* (D. APPLETON AND COMPANY, 1922), Chapter I. Philosophy he believes to be essentially metaphysics, and metaphysics aims to reduce the whole universe to a first principle. "Every special science," he says, "and every special form of practical activity interprets the facts of experience from some limited and one-sided or abstract point of view. *Metaphysics aims to correct these abstractions.*" (p. 3) Again, "inasmuch as the special sciences, such as physics, biology, psychology, and sociology, set out from unexamined dogmatic assumptions and issue, severally, in various uncoordinated results which require synthesis, in order to yield a consistent world view, to metaphysics belongs the twofold task of critically examining the primary assumptions of the sciences and of synthesizing their conclusions into a harmonious whole." (p. 2)

A popular statement of the same general conception will be found in B. A. G. Fuller's *History of Greek Philosophy* (HENRY HOLT AND COMPANY, 1923), Chapter I. The chapter is exceptionally readable for a discussion of so recondite a subject as the nature of philosophy and can hardly fail to prove suggestive to those interested in the question. A taste of the position and the style may be conveyed in this passage:

> To put it all in terms of the detective agency, the sciences are like the individual detectives following up and reporting upon that particular aspect of the case to which each has been assigned, whereas philosophy is like the chief who gathers all their reports together, reflects upon them, tries to harmonize them where they conflict, and to supplement them by reasonable conjecture where they fail to connect or are unable to follow the clew further into the unknown. Thus it constructs, using their reports as its data, a theory regarding the true inwardness of the case which seems to it to throw some light, at least, upon the central mystery. (p. 17)

It is interesting to contrast with this position statements made by scientists. In his address before the mathematics-physics section of the British Association, President G. H. Hardy spoke of the embarrassment inseparable from the obligation to address a group representing different sciences even when they were so closely related as mathematics, physics, and astronomy. Only two alternatives seemed open to him. He could take refuge, he said, in a series of general propositions, such as the value of scientific method, the need for better organization of scientific education and research, and other worn-out truisms. These matters he could discuss without undue strain on his honesty or his hearers' credulity. But in that case he felt he could hardly hope to increase any person's respect for his field of mathematics or for mathematicians. The only other alternative was, he thought, to say something about the one subject on which he had something to say. (*Nature,* Vol. 10, 381 ff.)

The reason for this embarrassment is given in another presidential address, that of A. H. Brooks, before the Washington Academy of Science. "Berzelius" (the noted Swedish chemist who died in 1848), said Mr. Brooks, "is credited with the statement that he would probably be the last man who could know all chemistry, meaning thereby that the science had grown so large that it was becoming beyond the grasp of any single mind. Since his day the naturalist has been supplanted by the botanist, zoölogist, and geologist. These have given way to the taxonomist, pathologist, ecologist, glaciologist, and paleontologist, to name but a few of the present subdivisions of the older professions. The end is not in sight, for as science becomes more exact a still higher degree of specialization is certain. Now a scientist may not even know the meaning of a word that describes the work of a professional colleague." (*Journal Wash. Acad. of Sci.*, Vol. 12, 83 *f.*)

A modified form of philosophic wholeness is championed by R. F. A. Hoernle, *Studies in Contemporary Metaphysics* (HARCOURT, BRACE AND HOWE, 1920), Chap. I. A criticism of this view appeared in *The Monist*, Vol. XXXIII, 438 *ff.*, and *The Journal of Philosophy*, Vol. XX, 309 *ff.*

A very good presentation of the conception of philosophy which parts company with this tradition is presented in John Dewey's *Reconstruction in Philosophy* (HENRY HOLT AND COMPANY, 1920), Chapter I, especially. Dewey's view is suggested in the following citation from the conclusion of that chapter.

When it is acknowledged that under disguise of dealing with ultimate reality, philosophy has been occupied with the precious values embedded in social traditions, that it has sprung from a clash of social ends and from a conflict of inherited institutions with incompatible contemporary tendencies, it will be seen that the task of future philosophy is to clarify men's ideas as to the social and moral strifes of their own day. . . . Philosophy which surrenders its somewhat barren monopoly of dealing with Ultimate and Absolute Reality will find a compensation in enlightening the moral forces which move mankind and in contributing to the aspirations of men to attain to a more ordered and intelligent happiness.

CHAPTER II

The Two Ideals

A very excellent paper, germane to the topic treated in this chapter, was contributed to the *Yale Review* by John Galsworthy. It is called "Castles in Spain," and it appeared as the opening article of Vol. XI (N.S.).

(39) Bertrand Russell's remarks in regard to possessions, etc., are from the chapter on "Property" in his *Principles of Social Reconstruction* (GEORGE ALLEN & UNWIN, 1918), or *Why Men Fight* (THE CENTURY CO., 1917).

Any person seriously interested in social reconstruction should by all means familiarize himself with the first chapter of that book. I cite a single passage, but the whole chapter (as indeed the whole book) has the most direct bearing on the problem of a better kind of social ideal:

There are three forces on the side of life which require no exceptional mental endowment, which are not very rare at present, and might be very common under better social institutions. They are love, the instinct of constructiveness, and the joy of life. All three are checked and enfeebled at present by the conditions under which men live—not only the less outwardly fortunate, but also the majority of the well-to-do. Our institutions rest upon injustice and authority: it is only by closing our hearts against sympathy and our minds against truth that we can endure the oppressions and unfairnesses by which we profit. Our economic system compels almost all men to carry out the purposes of others rather than their own, making them feel impotent in action and only able to secure a certain modicum of passive pleasure. All these things destroy the vigor of the community, the expansive affections of individuals, and the power of viewing the world generously. All these things are unnecessary and can be ended by wisdom and courage. If they were ended, the impulsive life of men would become wholly different, and the human race might travel towards a new happiness and a new vigor (pp. 23-24).

For a penetrating study of the nature and development of ideals, the reader is referred to B. H. Bode's *Fundamentals of Education* (THE MACMILLAN COMPANY, 1921), Chapter IV.

No thoroughgoing consideration of a better utilization of human impulses than we are making at present can afford, in my judgment, to neglect the contribution made by John Dewey in his book, *Human Nature and Conduct* (HENRY HOLT AND COMPANY, 1922), and R. H. Tawney in *The Sickness of Acquisitive Society*. (Published in America by HARCOURT, BRACE AND HOWE, 1920, under the title, *The Acquisi-*

tive Society). In the former, perhaps the most pertinent single portion is Part II, Chapter III.

CHAPTER III

Right for Right's Sake

(58) A. Clutton-Brock's book, *The Ultimate Belief* (CONSTABLE & CO., LTD., 1916), issuing out of feelings aroused by the war, is naturally colored by the prevailing psychology. It is, however, an extraordinary production, for it puts the argument in favor of the absolute and abstract nature of loyalty to the good, the true, the beautiful (which we have become accustomed to associate with heavy tomes to be understood only by the very learned) in a brief, lucid, direct, and persuasive form. Books like it are rare.

The American edition (E. P. DUTTON AND COMPANY, 1916) has an Introduction by Lyman Abbott. It is significant that in the very endorsement of the doctrine of right for right's sake, etc., the introduction suggests that in the concrete this abstract loyalty means adherence to specific conduct. One could not, it seems, do right for right's sake and fail to stand by the family as the basis of society, or refuse to believe in the purposive nature of the world. There is nothing odd in this. As we have seen, abstract morality must become concrete in application. I only call attention to this as another illustration of how the theory works in practice.

Immanuel Kant's philosophy of morality may be gained from his *Metaphysics of Morality* and his *Critique of Practical Reason*. It would be proper to refer the reader to these studies, or to T. K. Abbott's *Kant's Critique of Practical Reason and Other Works on the Theory of Ethics* (LONGMANS, GREEN & CO., 1889). But a summary of his position, as presented in some good history of philosophy, is likely to be much more serviceable. Richard Falckenberg, *History of Modern Philosophy* (HENRY HOLT AND COMPANY, 1893), pp. 383-400, gives the essential material in what seems to me the most satisfactory form.

Those who wish to consult Kant's own works will do well to choose what is known as Watson's Selections from Kant.

This book, John Watson's *The Philosophy of Kant, as Contained in Extract from His Own Writings* (JAMES MACLEHOSE AND SONS, 1919), is excellent in every respect. The selections are made by a Kantian scholar and the translation from the German is the best we have.

(68) The relevant literature on Treitschke (easily found under his name) must be read with judgment. The war aroused interest in Treitschke's political philosophy and this led to the publication of collections of extracts from his lectures. I have no cause to defend his point of view, but it does seem to me desirable to make a serious attempt to discover what his views were, if one pretends to give them. This has not been done. Obnoxious as his political program will appear to most Americans, there can be no doubt that it was impelled by a very lofty idealism. It is not impossible (strange as it may seem) that what divides us from him is just this idealism and the fact that we refuse to make the assumptions which are implicit in *our* nationalism as explicit as he was willing to make those involved in *his* nationalism.

(69) The present discussion of Bernhardi is based upon his little volume *Germany and the Next War* (LONGMANS, GREEN AND CO., 1914). Another book to be consulted is F. A. J. Von Bernhardi, *Germany and England* (G. W. DILLINGHAM, 1915).

(75) The moral theory touched upon at the conclusion of the chapter is touched upon again in Chapter IV, and is more fully treated in Chapter V.

The student who wishes to follow up the issue raised in this chapter should read John Dewey's *German Philosophy and Politics* (HENRY HOLT AND COMPANY, 1915). I had not read this book when the article "Kant and the Militarists" (of which the present chapter is a revision) was originally written.

CHAPTER IV

Might Makes Right

(77) Thrasymachus's contention, that justice is synonymous with the will of the stronger, appears in Book I, x, of Plato's *Republic*.

Nietzsche is frequently put on this side—which is a mistake. Nietzsche had an ideal, a very lofty ideal, other than might. But this is not a simple question. For elucidation one should turn to a study of Nietzsche. By far the best study that I know of in English (most of what has been printed on the subject in America being extremely shallow and distorted) is W. A. Salter, *Nietzsche, the Thinker* (HENRY HOLT AND COMPANY, 1917). See especially Chapter XXVII and pp. 340-344.

Almost any day one may read news stories or editorials in the daily press, or articles in the more popular periodicals, which prove beyond question that very many Americans agree substantially with Thrasymachus. All those who believe in virtue by intimidation belong to this class, as do the thousands whose moral theory rests on the faith that a God of Vengeance will ultimately cause all wrongdoers to suffer the consequences of their evil deeds. For many people God makes right by might.

A most direct and able argument for the proposition that might makes right is from the pen of E. B. McGilvary. It is called "The Warfare of Moral Ideals," and may be found in *The Hibbert Journal*, Vol. XIV, pp. 43-64.

Justice Oliver Wendell Holmes defends the same general position in a brilliant article entitled "Natural Law" in the *Harvard Law Review*, Vol. XXXII, pp. 40-44. This drew a reply from B. H. Bode, who in his paper, "Justice Holmes on Natural Law and the Moral Ideal," in *The International Journal of Ethics*, Vol. XXIX, pp. 397-404, subjects the contention to a searching examination.

Josiah Royce discussed the issue in *The Religious Aspect of Philosophy* (HOUGHTON, MIFFLIN COMPANY, 1885, 1913) Chapter III.

Another discussion which has a bearing on the topic is an article entitled "Morality the Last of the Dogmas," by Antonio Llano, in *The Philosophical Review*, Vol. V, pp. 371-394. The quotation on page 110 is a good sample of his position.

A study of how "the spirit of reform" has for centuries operated to bring "our system of law more and more into harmony with moral principles" was contributed to the *Har-*

vard Law Review, Vol. XXII, pp. 97-113, by James Barr Ames.

Perhaps the best thing to read in connection with this chapter is W. M. Leiserson's article, "The Way to Industrial Peace" in *The American Review*, Vol. II, p. 252. Mr. Leiserson makes very clear the contrast between coercion and adjustment as a practical method of dealing with conflicts of interests.

CHAPTER V

Right by Agreement

(109) The citation from Thomas Dwight, *Thoughts of a Catholic Anatomist* (LONGMANS, GREEN & Co., 1912), is from pp. 4-5.

(110) The Llano quotation is from the article on "Morality the Last of the Dogmas," *Philosophical Review*, Vol. V, pp. 377, 379.

(111) Emerson's words are from his "Lecture on the Times," printed in *Nature Addresses and Lectures*. The essays on the "Oversoul" and "Compensation" are involved in the interpretation here given of Emerson's view.

(115) The reference to James is to his address, "The Moral Philosopher and the Moral Life," printed in *The Will to Believe* (LONGMANS, GREEN & Co., 1896, etc.). I owe much to this discussion, though I came to it regrettably late in the development of the theory here presented.

(125) John Stuart Mill made the remark about the pig and Socrates in *Utilitarianism* (there are various editions), Chapter II, paragraph 6. Paul Janet's criticism is in his *Theory of Morals* (CHARLES SCRIBNER'S SONS, 1883), pp. 17-18, and E. B. McGilvary's criticism appeared in *The Hibbert Journal*, Vol. XIV, p. 62.

(129) John Dewey's endorsement of loyalty to the better aspects of the existing environment is from *Human Nature and Conduct* (HENRY HOLT AND COMPANY, 1922), p. 21. The student should also consult Chapter VII in the same author's *Reconstruction in Philosophy* (HENRY HOLT AND COMPANY, 1920).

For light on the relation of egoism and altruism the reader is directed to F. C. Sharp's thoroughgoing study, "Some Problems in the Psychology of Egoism and Altruism," *The Journal of Philosophy,* Vol. XX, pp. 85-104.

<h2 style="text-align:center">CHAPTER VI</h2>

<h3 style="text-align:center">The Self</h3>

(133) The Samuel Butler quotation is from *Unconscious Memory* (E. P. DUTTON & Co., 1911), pp. 78-79.

One of the very best discussions of the subject, at once profound in thought and remarkably clear in presentation, is Edward Carpenter's essay, "The Nature of the Self." It is in the appendix of his *Pagan and Christian Creeds* (HARCOURT, BRACE AND HOWE, 1920). The quotation here used is from this essay.

(135) Hume's discussion is in *A Treatise of Human Nature,* Book I, Part IV, par. 6.

(139) The quotation beginning, "What I believe to be my earliest memory," is from H. B. Alexander's *Nature and Human Nature* (THE OPEN COURT PUBLISHING COMPANY, 1923), p. 252.

(140) The illustration taken from Edmund Gosse's *Father and Son* (CHARLES SCRIBNER'S SONS, 1913) is from p. 36 *ff.*

William James should of course be consulted on this subject. The present reference is to *The Principles of Psychology* (HENRY HOLT AND COMPANY, 1902), Vol. I, pp. 291, 292. The whole discussion (Chapter X) is a psychological classic. But the *Varieties of Religious Experience* (LONGMANS, GREEN & Co., 1908) should also be consulted, especially Chapter VIII, "The Divided Self."

Edward Bok in *The Americanization of Edward Bok* (CHARLES SCRIBNER'S SONS, 1922) gives expression to a very common experience (which has, however, puzzled philosophers a great deal) when, as the writer of his own biography, he refers to the subject of his sketch in these words:

It is easy, therefore, for me to write of him as a personality apart; in fact, I could not depict him from any other point. To write of him in the first person, as if he were myself, is impossible, for he is not.

I have again and again found myself watching with intense amusement and interest the Edward Bok of this book at work. (pp. vii, viii)

Light is thrown on the subject of divisions in personality by such studies as Morton Prince's "The Dissolution of a Personality" (LONGMANS, GREEN & COMPANY, New York, 1906).

In addition to the real, original, or normal self [says Dr. Prince in introducing the subject referred to as Miss Christine L. Beauchamp] she may be any one of three different persons. I say three different, because, although making use of the same body, each, nevertheless, has a distinctly different character; a difference manifested by different trains of thought, by different views, beliefs, ideals, and temperament, and by different acquisitions, tastes, habits, experiences, and memories. . . . Two of these personalities have no knowledge of each other or the third, excepting such information as may be obtained by inference or second hand, so that in the memory of each of these two there are blanks which correspond to the times when the others are in the flesh. . . . Only one of the three has knowledge of the lives of the others, and this one presents such a bizarre character, so far removed from the others in individuality, that the transformation from one of the other personalities to herself is one of the most striking and dramatic features of the case. The personalities come and go in kaleidoscopic succession, many changes often being made in the course of twenty-four hours. And so it happens that Miss Beauchamp, if I may use the name to designate several distinct people, at one moment says and does and plans and arranges something to which a short time before she most strongly objected, indulges tastes which a moment before would have been abhorrent to her ideals, and undoes or destroys what she had just laboriously planned and arranged. (pp. 1-2)

(148) On the subject of the *real* self, I may add to the two quotations given, namely, W. H. Hudson, *A Hind in Richmond Park* (E. P. DUTTON AND COMPANY, 1923), p. 35, and William James, *Letters* (THE ATLANTIC MONTHLY PRESS,

1920), Vol. I, pp. 199-200, an interesting statement by Rousseau:

What I regret is not having kept a journal of my travels, being conscious that a number of interesting details have slipped my memory; for never did I exist so completely, never live so thoroughly, never was so much myself, if I may dare to use the expression, as in those journeys made on foot. Walking animates and enlivens my spirits; I can hardly think when in a state of inactivity; my body must be exercised to make my judgment active. The view of a fine country, a succession of agreeable prospects, the open air, a good appetite, and the health I gain by walking; the freedom of inns, and the distance from everything that can make me recollect the dependence of my situation, conspire to free my soul, and give boldness to my thoughts, throwing me, in a manner, into the immensity of existence, where I combine, choose, and appropriate all to my fancy, without constraint or fear. I dispose of all nature as I please; my heart, wandering from object to object, approximates and unites with those that please it, is surrounded by charming images, and becomes intoxicated with delicious sensations. *Confessions of Rousseau* (GIBBINGS AND COMPANY, 1907), pp. 166-167.

CHAPTER VII

Science and the Higher Life—The Renewal of Warfare

(157) The article "Drift" was written by R. K. Hack, and printed in *The Atlantic Monthly,* Vol. 118, p. 351 *ff.;* and the editorial in criticism of it in *The New Republic* is in Vol. 8, 237 *ff.*

(159) *Pro Vita Monastica* (ATLANTIC MONTHLY PRESS, 1923) is H. D. Sedgwick's contribution to the movement, grown to considerable proportions, which proposes to solve the problem of living in these perturbed times by withdrawing into some sequestered retreat. Mr. Sedgwick's manner of withdrawal is only for those who have sufficient means at their disposal to disregard the economic aspect of the problem.

(160) "Whither" was first printed in *The Atlantic Monthly,* Vol. 115, pp. 300-315. It was published as a booklet by HOUGHTON, MIFFLIN COMPANY, in 1915. The citations here made are easily found, and should be read in their setting.

The verse on page 163 is from *Recent Development of Physical Science,* Whetham, W. C. D. (P. BLAKISTON SON AND COMPANY, 1904), p. 10.

(164) Mr. Millikan's declaration of harmony between science and religion is obtainable in several forms. It was printed in *Science,* Vol. LVII, p. 631; and is published as a pamphlet by the American Institute of Sacred Literature, Hyde Park, Chicago, Illinois.

(166) The John Adams quotation is from his *Works,* Vol. X, p. 67 *ff.*

(171) The argument by V. T. Thayer, that the question of harmony between religious beliefs and scientific conclusions depends upon the way these terms are defined, is from an editorial in *The American Review,* Vol. I, p. 618. It is very clear from the literature on the subject that this is a fact which has been generally ignored, in spite of its direct and important bearing on the subject.

CHAPTER VIII

Science and the Higher Life—The Issue Developed

(174) Josiah Royce's straightforward statement of the relation of human interests to the universe as pictured by science is from his book, *William James and Other Essays* (THE MACMILLAN COMPANY, 1911), p. 65.

Edwin E. Slosson expresses himself similarly and with a touch of bitterness:

Admire Nature? Possibly, but be not blinded to her defects. Learn from Nature? We should sit humbly at her feet until we can stand erect and go our own way. Love Nature? Never! She is our treacherous and unsleeping foe, ever to be feared and watched and circumvented, for at any moment and in spite of all our vigilance she may wipe out the human race by famine, pestilence or earthquake and within a few centuries obliterate every trace of its achievement. *Creative Chemistry* (THE CENTURY Co., 1923), p. 10.

A good example of mechanistic science popularized is Ellwood Hendrick's paper, "A Plea for Materialism," *The At-*

lantic Monthly, Vol. 112, p. 342 *ff.* The quotations referring to men as machines are from this paper.

(177) Samuel Butler's more extensive discussion of machines and life is found in his *Erewhon.* The present brief citation is from *The Note Books of Samuel Butler* (A. C. FIFIELD, 1918), pp. 45-46. Many people have lately come to take his whimsical irony quite seriously.

(179) The quotation from George Gissing is from *The Private Papers of Henry Ryecroft,* the division Winter, section XVIII. The whole section breathes dread of science, especially the kind of science which he calls blatant and ubiquitous, which makes millionaires, and which leaves him nothing to do but to run away from it, and to take refuge in the thought that he has had "no part in bringing the tyrant to his throne."

(182) R. K. Duncan's statement of atomism is from *The New Knowledge* (A. S. BARNES & Co., 1906), pp. 15-16. The last paragraph of the chapter (omitted in the quotation) introduces a qualifying phrase. This does not change the real nature of the position taken, but it does confuse matters. Here it is:

Consequently whether we consider the atoms as the starting place in our search for the One Thing, or whether we think of them only as the foundation of all physical action and being, they are the most important things in the world to us, for they *are* us, physically at least, and any knowledge concerning them or any relation between them has, therefore, to us poor people they condition, an interest that is tragic. (p. 16)

In the same manner, Mr. Hendrick, having throughout his paper urged his readers to regard men and women as machines or apparatuses, at the end softens his mechanism to say: "Not a thing that has been said in this essay is a denial of the human soul. You are you and I am I, and within us both is the Mystery" (*Atlantic,* Vol. 112, p. 348). But for ambiguities of this sort the bearing of science on the higher life would have been better understood.

(184) The position of Jacques Loeb, as here given, is based on the first chapter of his book, *The Mechanistic Conception of Life* (THE UNIVERSITY OF CHICAGO PRESS, 1912),

and a paper entitled "Mechanistic Science and Metaphysical Romance," in *The Yale Review*, Vol. IV, p. 766 *ff.* (N.S.).

To these references may be added a note, "The Mechanistic Problem," in *The Monist*, Vol. XXIII, p. 148 *ff.*, and an excellent review of Mr. Loeb's book, in the same volume of *The Monist*, pp. 152-158.

The reader is more especially referred to two brief but intimate biographical sketches of Mr. Loeb, in *Science*, Vol. LIX, pp. 427-430.

CHAPTER IX

Science and the Higher Life—Looking Towards Harmony

The question discussed in this and the two preceding chapters is by many people thought to constitute the outstanding problem of present civilization. Mr. Soddy expresses a very general conviction when he says that the world is doomed "if it fools with the achievements of science as it has fooled too long in the past." It is therefore deplorable that in the debate which has centered around this problem of science and the higher ends of life, the spokesmen for science have indulged in vagueness and ambiguity. Words like those of R. H. Lowie, in his review of H. H. Newman's *Readings in Evolution,* are as rare as they are refreshing. Referring to the statement in this book that the "writer has been at some pains to make it clear that evolution and religion are strictly compatible," Mr. Lowie remarks: "We have no right to lull our wards into fancied security. Let us speak to them ingenuously, if at all: 'Evolution and religion are strictly compatible for some minds. We do not seek to undermine your faith; but we shall teach you science, whether it undermines your faith or not.'" (*The New Republic,* Vol. XXX, p. 26.)

Men of science have won a deserved recognition for persevering dedication to the search for objective truth, and they must be credited with having devised the most accurate methods of investigation as yet achieved by men; yet in the present-day movement to redefine the higher life their influence must be counted on the side of emotionalism and obscurantism. There are scientists of whom this cannot truthfully be said, but the great majority of those who have attempted to exert·an influence have taken this compromising position: they have stood unswervingly for the elimination of every form of obscurantism from science, while they have not only been willing to retain, but have insisted upon retaining, obscurantism and subjectivism in the moral and religious fields. Perhaps this has seemed necessary to them in order to "sell" science to the public. If so, the bargain may turn out to have cost a pretty price.

This phase of the subject has been excellently discussed in an article which appeared too late to be referred to in the body of this book. It is a pleasure to call attention to it, and to quote a paragraph which puts the problem with extraordinary acumen and with quite unusual lucidity and frankness. The article is by Ralph W. Nelson, and it is found in *The American Journal of Sociology*, Vol. XXIX, p. 553 *ff*. The portion referred to in particular runs as follows:

Now that universities and foundations, as scientific institutions, have achieved such prominence in our social life, they become a distinct temptation to scientists to seek the short cut of promulgating their doctrines by virtue of the authority of their respective institutions. While such an expedient may be excusable, or even advisable, as a temporary measure to win popular support for a specific issue, it is well for scientists to realize that it is a reversion to pre-scientific logic, which, if overworked, may readily defeat their larger purpose. What will doubtless be recorded as a classic instance of twentieth-century scientist's reverting to the method of authority is the recent testimonial against Bryan, that science is not antagonistic to religion, which was broadcasted in the daily press over the signatures of an imposing array of scientists and scientific-spirited preachers and theologians. This document may have been necessary to stem the tide toward educational obscurantism; but it is nothing more than an appeal to the authority of prominent names, and, hence, puts the men who signed it in a light compromisingly comparable to the position of those who dogmatize by virtue of their authority as representatives of institutionalized religion. (p. 557)

Two recent books of exceptional merit deal with the possible future effect of science on life. *Daedalus,* by J. B. S.

Haldane, puts the case hopefully, while *Icarus,* by Bertrand Russell, is a forecast of possibly sinister influences of Science on the world's future. Both books are published by E. P. DUTTON AND COMPANY.

(195) J. Arthur Thomson's view of the matter is taken, as indicated, from the book, *Introduction to Science* (HENRY HOLT AND COMPANY, 1911), the chapter on "Science and Religion." For a more extensive treatment, the student may consult the same author's *The Bible of Nature* (CHARLES SCRIBNER'S SONS, 1908), Chap. V, and *The System of Animate Nature* (HENRY HOLT AND COMPANY, 1920), Vol. I, Chapter I, and Vol. II, p. 649 *ff*.

(200) Although the position ascribed to Mr. Millikan was developed from an article contributed to the *Christian Century,* the same material is now more accessible in the form of a pamphlet issued by The American Institute of Sacred Literature, Hyde Park, Chicago, Illinois.

(210, 215) The quotations from E. W. Hobson are from his book, *The Domain of Natural Science* (THE MACMILLAN COMPANY, 1913), pp. 6, 77, 82, 30, 26, 28, 29. Chapter I is well worth reading as a whole in this connection.

(211) Frederick Soddy's warning is from *Science and Life* (E. P. DUTTON AND COMPANY, 1920), p. 36.

(214) Karl Pearson's conception of laws of nature is taken from *The Grammar of Science* (ADAM AND CHARLES BLACK, 1911). The quotations are from pp. 77, 82, and 30. But the whole of Chapter V should be read, and it is difficult to refrain from quoting these words beginning on p. 91:

> The reason we find in natural phenomena is surely put there by the only reason of which we have any experience, namely, the human reason. The mind of man in the process of classifying phenomena and formulating natural law introduces the element of reason into nature, and the logic man finds in the universe is but the reflection of his own reasoning faculty. A dog, if able to recognize the instinct which guides his actions, might very naturally suppose instinct and not reason to be the basis of natural phenomena, reflecting his own source of action into all he observed around him. Indeed, it seems to me more logical to find instinct than to find reason behind the setting and rising of the sun, for instinct at least does not presuppose consciousness. Perhaps if our dog were a Stoic dog the instinct would seem to him

inherent in the universe itself, while had he been reared at the parsonage he would certainly fancy his kennel the product of an instinct supercanine.

Chapter X

The Soul

Books and articles dealing with the soul are almost endless in number. Very different concepts are presented in the following three books:

Lafargue, Paul. *The Origin and Evolution of the Idea of the Soul:* a small book of 127 pages, published by Charles H. Kerr and Company, 1922. No orthodox Christian will like this treatment of the subject.

Steven, George. *The Psychology of the Christian Soul.* This book represents the Christian orthodox theological view. It is published by Hodder and Stoughton, 1911.

Hopkins, E. W. *The Origin and Evolution of Religion,* published by the Yale University Press, 1923. Chapter IX is of special interest as throwing light on the general meaning of soul and its various localizations in the human body.

A few additional definitions of the soul from the student papers referred to are perhaps called for, to guard against a too biased selection. It should be made clear that while the soul concept with which the past generations have been most familiar is losing its place of authority, very few college students go so far as to deny the existence of soul altogether. The answers here added are typical of others of the same tenor:

I *know* I have a soul. I do not *know* what it is. No one does. People can only give *opinions* about it, for the soul is too fine a structure to be analyzed or picked to pieces like other organs of the body. Having been made by superhuman hands for a most spiritual purpose, man is foolish to worry about its nature. He had better make it his chief aim to save that soul from eternal damnation.

I'm sure I have a soul because I have a strong conscience. The soul is the basis of this conscience and it is responsible for the morality that I have. If it were not for this so-called soul or conscience I'd fear for my moral life. The soul contains the inner thoughts and inspires the brain. God finds his way to us through the soul. Even those who have no religion may have a soul, but it doesn't function.

I really can't say positively "yes" or "no" to this question. I am at present groping for some truth regarding it. In my earlier years I believed I had a soul, but my trend of thought now tends to emphasize the non-existence of the soul as anything spiritual. The soul, I am coming to think, is physical, capable of disease or injury, just as the mind or consciousness is, to which it is closely related. This conviction of mine is derived from facts we know about insanity, recovery from insanity, and the effect of physical disturbances upon the state of the mind and soul.

Here's a guess at the "soul" proposition: your soul is that part of your mental processes which is concerned with ideals; the moral side (in a broad sense) of your mental life. It is very closely connected with your emotions, and consequently of great influence on your actions.

The large percentage of people have no soul. It is a characteristic of such rare persons as Jane Addams—who are so absorbed in doing some great good that they forget about themselves, as far as the material phase of life is concerned. The soul, in other words, is the really spiritual part of oneself—the part that follows some great vision and refuses to be discouraged by the obstacles that are usually too much for the ordinary man.

Chapter XI

The War and the God-Makers

Perhaps it should be repeated that the movement discussed in this chapter is not without historical antecedents. Even the change in the God-concept in response to a growing sense of democracy had been impressively discussed before the war gave rise to the more immediate venture. The following passages are of especial interest in this connection; the first from a paper by Robert Archey Woods, the second from a paper by Harry Allen Overstreet:

It has been said that at the heart of democratic association, forming the source of its power, is the peculiar principle by which the whole is more than the sum of its parts. The output of two men working together is more than the total of what they produce separately. The combination of intelligence, the coalescence of wills, is in itself a third and compelling factor. This

economic surplus value has its realizable and its realized counterpart in the relations of the inner life. Jesus said: "Where two or
three are gathered together in my name, there am I in the midst
of them." . . . A surplus value of the spirit, a power not ourselves, is evidenced in the process and in the result of every fresh
extension of active fraternity toward the moral upbuilding of
society. . . . In any estimate of the present meaning of democracy, the road which it is to travel, and the length which it is to
go, the religious afflatus—rising, vaguely understood, but soon to
be overpowering—must be taken account of more deeply than
anything else.

The new spirit, forming itself, as it were, upon the restless
sea of humanity, will without doubt determine the future sense
of God and destiny. The deistic conception of an age now completely past, that God is some distant monarch, will fade into the
darkness with the social system which gave it rise; and society
as a federal union, in which each individual and every form of
human association shall find free and full scope for a more
abundant life, will be the large figure from which is projected
the conception of God in whom we live and move and have our
being. Under such a conception it will be found and felt that
at every one of all the points in the never-ending complexity of
human affairs where one life touches another, there is a sacra-
mental relationship which is being either reverenced or defiled.

These paragraphs are from Mr. Woods's able paper,
"Democracy a New Unfolding of Human Power," in *Studies
in Philosophy and Psychology*, by former students of Charles
Edward Garman (HOUGHTON, MIFFLIN COMPANY, 1906), pp.
97-99. Mr. Overstreet's, which follow, are from an article
entitled "The Democratic Conception of God," in *The Hil-
bert Journal*, Vol. XI, p. 394 *ff*. It is the best discussion of
the subject known to me:

It is true of philosophy, as of other disciplines, that necessity
is the mother of invention. Philosophy exists to serve human
needs. As needs change, taking new shape and direction, philosophy undergoes corresponding transformation. . . . It follows,
then, that if the present age in some deep-reaching way has set
a new problem, has set a new "practical thoughtfulness," philosophy must be alive to these altered needs (p. 394).

We are coming therefore to the new thought that society is
guided—if we may still use that word—not by king or class, but

by the infinite action and reaction of all its members. This new conception of society *making itself,* lifting itself through its very imperfections—through the struggle of these one with another—to planes of more effective realization, must obviously have profound bearing *upon the manner in which we shall view the process of the total universe.* Must it not change profoundly our hitherto typical way of regarding the organization of the world? What, in short, is to be the new world-view consonant with this democratic thought of a society *making itself?* (p. 402)

Consequently the God of the future is the figure of myriad lives, and yet of one vast group life, in ceaseless activity. There is no place in the figure for an eternally perfect being, and no need: no need, for the vast society by its own inherent mass-dialectic—of struggle and adaptation, coöperation and conflict—is working out its own destiny; no place, for the society, democratic from end to end, can brook no such radical class distinction as that between a supreme being favored with eternal and absolute perfection and the mass of beings doomed to the lower ways of imperfect struggle. It is . . . the conception of the God *that is ourselves,* in whom and of whom we literally are; the God that, in every act and intention, *we, with all our countless fellows, are realizing.* . . . It is a God that in one respect is in the making, growing with the growth of the world; suffering and sinning and conquering with it; a God, in short, that *is* the world in the spiritual unity of its mass-life. (pp. 409-410)

(247) The Haydon quotation is from an article, "The Quest for God," in *The Journal of Religion,* Vol. III, p. 590. The article is an excellent historical survey of the meanings of God in the religious experience of men.

(252-256) G. A. Studdert Kennedy's book, *The Hardest Part,* was published by the YOUNG MEN'S CHRISTIAN ASSOCIATION (American Expeditionary Forces), Paris, 1918. References are to pages 34, 35 and 40.

(256) E. H. Reeman's book, *Do We Need a New Idea of God?,* was published by GEORGE W. JACOBS AND COMPANY, 1917. References are particularly to Chapters I and III, though not exclusively.

(259) The conversation referred to in connection with H. G. Wells is reported in *The New Republic,* Vol. IX, p. 234. Other references to Mr. Wells are readily accessible.

(267) The quotation from Galsworthy's *Saints Progress*

(CHARLES SCRIBNER'S SONS, 1919), is found on p. 42. There is much else of the same sort in the book.

One cannot but wonder, now that an anti-democratic tendency seems to have developed in various parts of the world, whether this is to be urged as the justification for a Fascisti conception of God, with Mussolini as model.

CHAPTER XII

The Hunger for Cosmic Support

The theory of Christian origins with which this chapter opens is not susceptible of nice logical demonstration. It is one of those convictions which is forced on a man's mind by the total drift of his acquaintance with relevant facts. Some years ago, when reading the Gospels, I was struck by the change from the word "life" to the word "soul" in these adjacent passages:

> For whosoever will save his life shall lose it; but whosoever shall lose his life for my sake and the gospels', the same shall save it.
> For what shall it profit a man, if he shall gain the whole world, and lose his own soul?
> Or what shall a man give in exchange for his soul?
>
> Mark 8: 35-37.

It seemed clear that the same thing was referred to in each case; then why this change in rendering?

Taking the matter a little further I discovered that for the word translated "soul" in the text of the authorized version, the margin offered "life"; that the revised version reversed this, putting "life" into the text and making "soul" optional; while *The Twentieth Century New Testament* (and other recent translations) dropped the term soul altogether. This naturally suggested looking the matter up in the Greek testament, to see whether "life" and "soul" were translations of the same or different words. It turned out that they were translations of the same word. Thus begun, the investigation continued, not systematically, but off and on as occasion offered, until eventually it led to the conception of Jesus and his mission which, in one way or another, has come to be

held by many people in our time. All of which, it goes
without saying, is not offered as proof for the correctness
of the conception; it is merely intended to help avoid misunderstanding.

Among the large and interesting literature bearing on the
subject, I especially wish to mention these items:

Burton, E. De W., "Spirit, Soul, and Flesh," Vol. III of
Historical and Linguistic Studies (UNIVERSITY OF CHICAGO
PRESS, 1918); Hart, R. L., *The Man Himself* (DOUBLEDAY,
PAGE AND COMPANY, 1923); France, Anatole, "The Pro-
curator of Judæa" in *The Mother of Pearl;* Zangwill, Israel,
Italian Fantasies (THE MACMILLAN COMPANY, 1910), Fan-
tasia Nepolitana; "A Gentleman with a Duster," *Seven Ages*
(S. P. PUTNAM'S SONS, 1923), Chapter III; Rauschenbusch,
W., *Christianity and the Social Crisis* (THE MACMILLAN
COMPANY, 1907), Chapter II; Foster, G. B., *The Finality
of the Christian Religion* (UNIVERSITY OF CHICAGO PRESS,
1909).

(282) John Fiske's religious interpretation of evolution is
from *The Destiny of Man* (HOUGHTON, MIFFLIN COMPANY),
p. 25.

(287) Gilbert Murray's essay, *The Stoic Philosophy,* for
some years out of print, is now to be had from the APPEAL
PUBLISHING COMPANY, Girard, Kansas. The part quoted is
on p. 41 of this booklet.

(288) John Dewey's statement that mankind has suffered
loss as a result of the belief that ideals must be transcendental, is in *Essays in Experimental Logic* (THE UNIVERSITY
OF CHICAGO PRESS, 1916), p. 72.

The author is not under the illusion that religion is fully
discussed in this chapter. He is aware that noble achievements in art, architecture, music, literature, and human personality must be credited to religion as the source. And it
is conceded that something more may be said of religious
emotion than is here said. This is evident from the statement on p. 262. All this, however, is believed to leave the
argument of the chapter untouched.

INDEX

320 INDEX